T0322432

Praise for *Training Camp*

"Inspiration on every page. I picked this
book up and couldn't put it back down. It
will help you become the best you can be."

—Mark Batterson, Lead Pastor, National Community Church;
Author, *In a Pit with a Lion on a Snowy Day*

"Training Camp is a winner. Reading this book has
inspired me to work harder, lead better, and leave a
lasting legacy. Once again, Jon delivers a message that
will have a life-changing impact on those who read it."

—Todd Gothberg, Vice President,
Volvo Construction Equipment

What the Best
Do Better
Than Everyone Else

Training
Camp

A Fable About Excellence

JON GORDON

WILEY

John Wiley & Sons, Inc.

Copyright © 2009 by Jon Gordon. All rights reserved.

Published by John Wiley & Sons, Inc., Hoboken, New Jersey.
Published simultaneously in Canada.

No part of this publication may be reproduced, stored in a retrieval system, or transmitted in any form or by any means, electronic, mechanical, photocopying, recording, scanning, or otherwise, except as permitted under Section 107 or 108 of the 1976 United States Copyright Act, without either the prior written permission of the Publisher, or authorization through payment of the appropriate per-copy fee to the Copyright Clearance Center, Inc., 222 Rosewood Drive, Danvers, MA 01923, (978) 750-8400, fax (978) 646-8600, or on the web at www.copyright.com. Requests to the Publisher for permission should be addressed to the Permissions Department, John Wiley & Sons, Inc., 111 River Street, Hoboken, NJ 07030, (201) 748-6011, fax (201) 748-6008, or online at http://www.wiley.com/go/permissions.

Limit of Liability/Disclaimer of Warranty: While the publisher and author have used their best efforts in preparing this book, they make no representations or warranties with respect to the accuracy or completeness of the contents of this book and specifically disclaim any implied warranties of merchantability or fitness for a particular purpose. No warranty may be created or extended by sales representatives or written sales materials. The advice and strategies contained herein may not be suitable for your situation. You should consult with a professional where appropriate. Neither the publisher nor author shall be liable for any loss of profit or any other commercial damages, including but not limited to special, incidental, consequential, or other damages.

For general information on our other products and services or for technical support, please contact our Customer Care Department within the United States at (800) 762-2974, outside the United States at (317) 572-3993 or fax (317) 572-4002.

Wiley also publishes its books in a variety of electronic formats. Some content that appears in print may not be available in electronic books. For more information about Wiley products, visit our web site at www.wiley.com.

Library of Congress Cataloging-in-Publication Data:

Gordon, Jon, 1971–
  Training camp : what the best do better than everyone else / by Jon Gordon.
    p. cm.
  Includes index.
  ISBN 978-0-470-46208-9 (cloth : acid-free paper)
  1. Success.   2. Struggle.   I. Title.
  BJ1611.2.G67 2009
  650.1–dc22

                                                        2009007452

Printed in the United States of America.

36   35   34   33   32   31   30   29

For Kathryn,

you give me strength.

For Jade and Cole,

*always strive to be your best and bring out the
best in others.*

Contents

Acknowledgments x
Introduction xiii
1 Kickoff 1
2 Ankle Sprain 5
3 Press Conference 7
4 Pain 9
5 The Phone Call 15
6 Treatment 19
7 Questions 23
8 On the Sideline 27
9 The Playbook 29
10 The Telescope 35
11 Continuous Improvement 43
12 The Benefits of a Coach 47
13 The Myth 51
14 The Game-Day Principle 53

15 Ten Percent Better   57

16 The Microscope   61

17 Mental Zoom-Focus   67

18 Patience   69

19 Mental Toughness   71

20 Twenty Ways to Get Mentally Tough   77

21 A Bad Day   81

22 Heal Strong   85

23 Feeling Better   89

24 Preparation   91

25 The Cut   93

26 Faith   97

27 The Fishing Trip   99

28 Story and Belief   105

29 Tests   107

30 Pressure   109

31 Seize the Moment   111

32 The Breaking Point   115

33 The Spotlight   125

34 Celebration   129

35 Final Cuts   131

36 Leave a Legacy   135

37	**The Day**	**139**
38	**The Coin**	**143**
39	**The Final Lesson**	**147**
40	**A New Beginning**	**151**

Appendixes	*155*
The Energy Bus Training Program	*157*
Other Books by Jon Gordon	*159*

Contents

Acknowledgments

I am thankful for all the people who have encouraged, empowered, and coached me through the training camp of life. Without them this book would not have been written.

Thank you to my wife Kathryn for bringing out the best in me. I'm thrilled that the lessons in this book have dramatically improved your performance on the tennis court. Wimbledon, here we come!

Thank you to my agent Daniel Decker, who has provided invaluable support over the years.

Thank you to Matt Holt, Shannon Vargo, and the amazing team at John Wiley & Sons for your skill, talent, hard work, and support. You are the best publishing team on the planet.

Thank you to the special coaches and teachers throughout my life—Ivan Goldfarb, Tony Ciozza, Ed Ehmann, and Richie Moran.

Thank you to Coach Mike Smith, Tony Boselli, Pete Carroll, Jeff Gordon, Danny Gans, Alvin Pearman, Tom

McManus, and many others for sharing your ideas and thoughts with me.

Thank you to Kathryn Gordon, Daniel Decker, Jennifer Malhotra, Christina Kisley, Jason Pogue, Mike Norris, and Ben Newman for reviewing the manuscript and helping me make it the best it could be.

Thank you to Erwin McManus, Rob Bell, and Ken Blanchard for guiding me on my faith journey. Your life example and your teachings have changed my life.

Most of all I'd like to thank the Father, the Son, and the Holy Spirit. You are the power behind my words, the creative genius behind this book, and the love that flows through me. You are the ultimate coach and trainer who has and continues to train me, mold me, and develop me to be my best and to bring out the best in others.

Introduction

B efore the 2008 NFL season, Mike Smith, the Jacksonville Jaguars' defensive coordinator, was hired to be the head coach of the Atlanta Falcons. They had won only four games the previous year and Coach Smith was charged with improving the culture and turning the team around. As summer approached, Coach Smith called me and told me that he was having all the coaches and players read my book *The Energy Bus: 10 Rules to Fuel your Life, Work, and Team with Positive Energy* and invited me to speak to the team during training camp. I had met Coach Smith the year before while speaking to the Jacksonville Jaguars during their 2007 training camp.

The same week that I was to speak to the Atlanta Falcons I was also scheduled to speak to a financial services company that was regarded by many as having the best sales team in the financial industry. As I prepared for these talks I thought a lot about what I should say that would benefit them. After all, I would be talking to people who had reached the pinnacle of their industry. On one hand you had the best football players in the world. On the other hand you had the best salespeople in the world.

As part of my preparation I interviewed the top salespeople from the financial services company and while I was expecting to hear some new sales techniques that I hadn't heard before, I discovered there wasn't any secret formula to their success. They told me they simply worked hard, focused on the fundamentals, stayed positive, and had a great desire to succeed and make an impact. These were the same things I had heard from the best professional athletes I knew and from all the people I had interviewed over the years that were considered the best in their field.

This inspired a series of thoughts about what makes someone great in their field of work. I discovered that the best of the best, whether they're salespeople, athletes, teachers, nurses, entrepreneurs, musicians, and so on, share a number of similar characteristics. There is a formula for success. There are things that the best do that others don't and things that they do better than everyone else. There is a way that the best of the best approach their life and work and craft that differentiates them from others. This formula is predictable, repeatable, and simple to understand, but it's a process and it requires initiative, dedication, focus, and loads of positive energy.

As I left the Falcons' training camp after my talk and headed to the airport, the idea for this book popped into my head. I heard the words *Training Camp* loud and clear, from God's mouth to my ears. I knew I was supposed to share the principles and lessons in this book, not with just athletes but with anyone in any field who strived to be their best. While this story takes place in a sports setting, I hope you realize it's a life story that applies to you, your team, your co-workers, your family and kids.

I have even shared the lessons from this book with my daughter, Jade, and son, Cole. My hope is that when they are in high school and college this book will serve as a playbook for their lives and inspire them to strive for excellence in whatever career path they choose.

In this spirit, as you go through the training camp of your life, I hope that wherever you are on your journey, that this book will also inspire you to strive to be your best and bring out the best in your team—your work team, your sports team, your family team, your church team, and your school team. After all, life is a team sport.

Leave a Legacy,
Jon

Chapter 1

Kickoff

 Martin Jones stood at the five-yard line waiting for the kickoff. He could feel the electricity in the air. The stadium was packed with 60,000 people—all screaming wildly—but Martin didn't hear a thing. His eyes were focused on the flight of the ball. His ears were filled with the sounds of his own breath and the perpetual thumping of his racing heart. The smell of fresh-cut grass reminded him of the hundreds of games, practices, and kickoffs that brought him to this very moment. He had played thousands of hours of football throughout his life, and yet he had never experienced a moment quite like this. It was the moment of all moments. It was his first pre-season game and as an undrafted rookie trying to make it in the NFL, this was his one shot to get noticed.

Veterans didn't have to get noticed. First-round draft picks with big signing bonuses didn't have to stand out. But undrafted nobodies had to do something special during the pre-season to catch the eye of the coaches, scouts, and key decision makers who would decide their fate. Every play, every moment, every movement mattered. This was his one shot to do something special, to make the statement that he had what it took to compete with the best football players in the world. A great play meant he would be on the team for at least another week. A mistake would surely mean the end of his dream. An average play . . . well, that wasn't an option for Martin. Playing it safe was never his style, and he wasn't about to start now. He was going to go for broke or fail trying. He owed it to his high school and college coaches. He owed it to his family. He owed it to himself.

And as Martin caught the kickoff, he made the most of his opportunity. He ran slowly to the left looking for an opening as 11 opposing tacklers raced toward him. When his blockers met the defense with fierce collisions, he cut to the right and saw the opening he was waiting for. It wasn't a big opening, but it was big enough for him to sprint through it into the open field. A player dove at his feet, but Martin was one step ahead. One person to beat and he was in the clear. The kicker, the last line of defense, ran straight toward him, but Martin made such a quick fake that the kicker fell to the ground and Martin ran past him.

All that could get between him and the end zone were two players chasing him. One dove and just missed his leg while the other closed in on him. Martin pumped his arms and legs as fast as he could and ran toward the end zone like a man shot from a cannon.

Seconds later he was celebrating a touchdown with his teammates in the end zone. He not only caught the eye of his coaches and thousands of fans, but he also electrified the crowd with his speed and athletic ability. Everyone but Martin was stunned.

Chapter 2

Ankle Sprain

When a player catches a coach's eye, the coach tends to give him more opportunities to show his stuff. This leads to success if the player is the "real deal," or failure if the player is a "one play" wonder. Coaches know that any player can look like a superstar on any given play, but the "real deals" have a knack for making great plays often. So it was no surprise that the coaches put Martin in at running back and called for him to get the ball on a screen pass. Expecting Martin to get crushed by the opposing tacklers, they were pleasantly surprised when he made a one-handed catch, broke two tackles, and outran the final defender into the end zone for another touchdown. Now everyone noticed Martin Jones.

But what no one noticed was that Martin turned and sprained his ankle while eluding the tacklers. The injury didn't stop him from scoring a touchdown—thanks to the adrenaline pumping through his body—but while he was standing on the sidelines after the play, his ankle quickly began to swell up and Martin knew he would have to let the trainer know the unfortunate news. He was done for the night. As Martin sat on the sidelines, shaking his head, the ankle got bigger and the pain grew worse. Martin only hoped it wasn't a serious injury. He knew all too well that it was very unlikely for an undrafted rookie to make the team, and the probability of an *injured* undrafted rookie making the team was *zero*.

When the game was over, Martin hopped on one leg to the training room to receive treatment for his ankle.

Chapter 3

Press Conference

 After the game, the head coach surveyed the room. Yes, the season was here. Another year of football, and this meant another year of stupid questions from reporters. While he wanted to tackle every single one of them, he had learned to play their game in a more civilized but skillful way. They would ask questions that would hopefully prompt the coach to make a statement or share a quote that would give them a headline or something negative to write about. The reporters feasted on controversy and negativity, and they loved when he and the team gave them plenty of it. The coach, however, had discovered the art of starving reporters. His answers were short, always positive, and focused on the future, not the past. He gave them enough info so that they could do their jobs but decided it was best for him and his team to do their talking on the football field, not in the media.

The media on this night, however, didn't want to talk about anything negative. They were far more interested in the positive performance of Martin Jones.

"Where did he come from?" they asked.

"A small Division 1 program," coach answered.

"How come no one ever heard of him?"

"Because he wasn't drafted. Every year there are guys who get invitations to training camp who aren't drafted. I used to coach with Martin's college coach and heard good things about him, so we decided to give him a shot."

"So he's a diamond in the rough?" one of the reporters asked.

"That remains to be seen," coach answered. "He made some great plays, but it was just one game. There's a lot of training camp left."

"How come he didn't play anymore after his second touchdown?" another reporter asked.

"I am told by the training staff that he sprained his ankle while running for his second touchdown."

"Is it serious?"

"We don't know yet."

"Will he make the team?"

"The jury is still out on that. A lot of guys have talent in this league, but you have to be able to withstand the wear and tear on your body that this game demands. Getting hurt during training camp is honestly not a good sign. It's a rough game and a long season. So we'll see. I have to run, guys. Thanks so much," coach said as he walked briskly out the media room door, thankful the media wanted to talk about Martin Jones and not the team's poor defensive performance.

Chapter 4

Pain

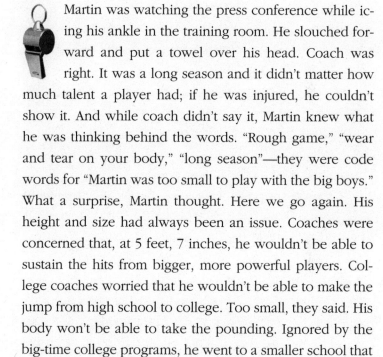

Martin was watching the press conference while icing his ankle in the training room. He slouched forward and put a towel over his head. Coach was right. It was a long season and it didn't matter how much talent a player had; if he was injured, he couldn't show it. And while coach didn't say it, Martin knew what he was thinking behind the words. "Rough game," "wear and tear on your body," "long season"—they were code words for "Martin was too small to play with the big boys." What a surprise, Martin thought. Here we go again. His height and size had always been an issue. Coaches were concerned that, at 5 feet, 7 inches, he wouldn't be able to sustain the hits from bigger, more powerful players. College coaches worried that he wouldn't be able to make the jump from high school to college. Too small, they said. His body won't be able to take the pounding. Ignored by the big-time college programs, he went to a smaller school that didn't measure him in terms of inches. Then when he became one of the top running backs in college football and set all kinds of school records, new critics and doubters emerged, saying the same old things. He was too small for the NFL. He wouldn't be able to sustain the hits. He won't be able to stay healthy. That's why he didn't get drafted. But it didn't bother Martin. He had spent his life proving the critics and doubters wrong. He knew that while they could measure the length of his body, they couldn't measure the size of his heart. All he needed was a chance, and now that chance was in jeopardy because of a stupid ankle injury.

"What do I do now?" Martin shouted in frustration.

"Now we wait and see how bad it is and how quick it heals," said Gus, the head athletic trainer, as he walked back into the training room.

"Sorry for yelling," Martin said as he tried to contain his anger. "I didn't think anyone was in here."

"It's okay. As you can tell from my hair and the wrinkles on my face, I've been an athletic trainer in this league a long time and I've seen my share of injuries, and they are never fun and always frustrating," he said with a thick New York accent.

"I just have to get back on that field. This is all I've got," he said as he punched the table he was sitting on.

"I know," answered Gus. "I know."

He did know. He had seen thousands of players come through training camp. Some came from the finest football programs in the country; others came from jobs bagging groceries and building houses. They came from farms in the Midwest, the streets of California, the bright lights of

Texas, and the suburbs of Florida. Some came with fame and fortune; others were so broke they had to sleep in their cars. Yet all of them came with their eyes wide open and a dream to play in the NFL. For some guys the dream came true. They made the team with only a dime to their names and in a few years they were household names, celebrity endorsers and multimillionaires. Others were not as fortunate. They came to training camp with a dream and left with a bruised body and a broken heart. Of those who failed to make the team, some would give up on their football careers, while others would keep their dream alive and make it eventually with another team or play in Canada. Gus had seen it all. He didn't know Martin, but he knew his story was like the stories of so many who came before him. He also knew that to help Martin he could do what he had done for the last 30 years for countless players: help him heal as quickly as possible, make him laugh, and share a word of encouragement. It was his role and he took pride in it. Gus looked at the ankle.

"See, the swelling is already coming down. Are you a fast healer?"

"Yes, always been. How long do you think I'll be out?"

"Hard to say. A few days. A week, tops. Good news is that it's not a high ankle sprain."

"A few days. A week," Martin said grimacing and shaking his head. "They'll probably cut me before then."

"I'm not so sure, Martin. You played great tonight. You might have made them curious. They may want to see

11

Pain

what else you can do before they make a decision to let you go. Besides, injuries are not all that bad. There's an upside, you know."

"Like what," said Martin who never heard anyone say anything positive about an injury before.

"Like the fact that an injury slows you down."

"Yeah, they really slow you down when you can't run on them," Martin said with a big smile and laugh. He was known for his big smile that he would flash during college games and afterward for the local media, but he smiled a lot less frequently these days.

"No, I mean they slow you down mentally so you can think more clearly," Gus said, chuckling. "Everyone comes to training camp and within the first day, their head is swirling with new rules and information, greater expectations and demands, and new strategies and techniques. Suddenly it feels like the earth is spinning faster and you're on one of those teacup rides in an amusement park. Frankly, the fast pace of life and football throws a lot of players off balance. There's so much to remember mentally and so much pressure to perform physically that players lose their way. So, my new friend, the upside is this: A minor injury and a few days off from the whirlwind is a great time to get refocused and think about what you truly want. It's a time to get your head right."

"But what good is having my head right if my leg won't move?" Martin said.

"Great point, but what good is having a healthy body if your mind is not in the game?" countered Gus. "While my job is to help athletes stay strong and healthy, I've been around enough of them to know that how you train the mind is actually more important than how you train the body. Everyone comes into this league with ability. Some have it more than others. But it's not ability that separates those who make the team from those who don't. It's sustainability. And sustainability has as much to do with mental strength and mental preparation as it does physical health. How you deal with an injury matters. How you deal with setbacks matters. How you focus and prepare matters. How you handle all the pressure of being in a fishbowl where everyone is watching your every move, that matters. I can get your ankle ready to play and your athletic ability can carry you in the short run, but it's your mind that will determine how well you perform in the long run. As Sun Tzu said, 'Every battle is won before it's ever fought.' It starts in the mind."

Martin nodded as he listened intently. It wasn't the first time he'd heard someone talk about the importance of a positive attitude. He had heard plenty of coaches talk about staying positive, and it seemed his mother's favorite phrase was "positive energy."

"So how about I focus on getting your ankle healed and you use this time to get your mind focused and ready so you can play at the top of your game. I'm telling you,

13

Pain

Martin, there is an upside and a blessing here. You just have to realize it."

"Sounds like a deal," Martin said, as he wished quietly to himself that it was as easy as Gus made it seem. He hadn't been in a good state of mind lately and he had a very good reason. And as Gus walked out of the treatment room to his office, "that reason" called Martin on his cell phone.

Chapter 5

The Phone Call

 Martin answered the phone as he looked around the training room to make sure everyone was gone. The voice on the other end of the line couldn't have been sweeter. It was the voice of the one who first and always loved him.

"Hey, Momma," Martin said.

"You were great tonight, Martin. We all watched you on television. I was cheering, 'That's my baby boy. He's playing in the NFL.'"

"Thanks, Momma," he said, unsure of whether he had the heart to tell her.

"Why didn't you play any more after your touchdown?" she asked.

Never one to lie to his mother, Martin knew he had to give her an answer. "Because I got injured. I sprained my ankle and I don't know what's going to happen now. I might not make the team. I'm scared. I'm real scared—We have to get your heart better. I don't know what else to do," he said as tears welled up in his eyes.

"You worry too much about me, Martin. I have my faith. God will provide."

"Well, he hasn't yet," Martin said, gritting his teeth as tears streamed down his face; he looked around the room to make sure no one was there.

"I'm going to get your heart fixed, Momma. Whatever it takes, I'm going to get it done."

"Oh, Martin, you've always been such a good boy. Always done the right thing. Always try to be so strong. Always trying to do it by yourself." She knew she never had to worry about Martin getting in trouble. He was the one who took care of his younger sister and brother. He was the one who made sure the family went to church on Sundays. He was the one who worked so hard in school and at football. But what worried her most about Martin was his lack of faith. He tried to do everything by himself so much that he left no room for miracles, she thought.

"I'm going to be fine," she said, trying to assure him. "You have to have faith, Martin. I have it. I have enough for the whole world, but you have to have it, too. God has a plan. He has one for me and he has one for you. God will provide for both of us. You just wait and see."

"I hope so, Momma. I really hope so. I just have to get better."

"You will, baby. You will. Just pray on it and remember you can't do it on your own. You're not that strong."

"Okay, Momma. Okay. I'll talk to you tomorrow. You get some rest. You sound tired," Martin said as he hung up the phone and placed a towel over his head to cover his face. It had been a year since she was diagnosed with a narrowing of the aortic valve. Every time he spoke to her she seemed more and more tired. The doctor said that the heart was being overworked as a result and surgery was absolutely necessary to avoid congestive heart failure. But the surgery was expensive and they didn't have insurance. Martin pleaded with several hospitals, but they wouldn't perform the surgery without the money to pay for it. Martin was angry at the system. He was angry at God, and he was angry at himself for getting injured. "I've got to get better," he repeated to himself.

Martin didn't think anyone was listening, but Gus heard Martin's conversation. Most of all he heard the despair in his voice. He picked up the phone in his office, dialed a number, and simply said, "Looks like we have another one. I'll see you tomorrow morning."

Chapter 6

Treatment

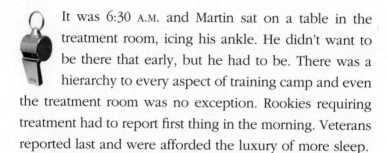 It was 6:30 A.M. and Martin sat on a table in the treatment room, icing his ankle. He didn't want to be there that early, but he had to be. There was a hierarchy to every aspect of training camp and even the treatment room was no exception. Rookies requiring treatment had to report first thing in the morning. Veterans reported last and were afforded the luxury of more sleep.

Martin had arrived before any of the other rookies, and he sat alone in silence, thinking about his two touchdowns the night before. He thought about his injury and, as always, his thoughts turned to getting his mother better. For the first time in his life he felt helpless and powerless. What do I do now, he wondered? He was in such deep thought that he didn't notice Coach Ken, the offensive line coach, approach him. When he finally snapped out of it he saw the tall, imposing man with a short gray buzz cut standing in front of him. Everyone knew about Coach Ken. He was an All-American in college and one of the best offensive linemen to ever play professional football. And yet as someone who had played the game weighing over 300 pounds, Coach Ken now resembled a tri-athlete more than an offensive lineman. He was tall, lean, and fit.

"How you doing, Martin?" he asked sincerely.

"Okay, Coach. Getting better every minute," he answered, flashing a big smile. "What are you doing here so early?"

"I'm an early riser. I like to get an early start on the day, and it also allows me to come down here and see how the players are doing. Great game last night, by the way. You really lit it up."

"Thanks. Now I just got to get better."

"Yeah, about that. When you are done with your treatment, come to my office. I'd like to talk to you about a few things."

"Okay," Martin answered anxiously as he wondered if he was about to be let go from the team.

His heart started to race as Coach Ken walked away and Gus approached.

Martin turned to Gus. "He wants to see me in his office. Do you think this is the end of the road for me?"

"I don't think so," answered Gus. "Like I said before, you probably got the coaches curious and he wants to get to know you better. And if I know Coach Ken, he probably has some advice for you."

"Advice . . . from Coach Ken? Are you serious?" asked Martin. "He hardly speaks."

"It's not how much you say. It's what you say when you say it that counts," Gus said. "Those who have the most profound things to say often speak the least. So if I were you, Martin, when he speaks, I'd listen up."

"Oh, you bet I'll listen to him. I'll listen to every word, especially if he's not going to cut me from the team," Martin said with a big smile.

"Good luck," Gus said, smiling and shaking his head as he walked away to deal with the other injured rookies who had just arrived.

Martin continued icing his ankle for another 10 minutes as he wondered what in the world Coach Ken wanted to talk to him about. Then he picked up his crutches and hobbled to the other side of the building to Coach Ken's office.

Chapter 7

Questions

 Martin stood nervously outside the door as he knocked.

"Come on in," a quiet voice said from inside.

Martin hobbled in and saw Coach sitting behind his desk, eating.

"Those look good," Martin said.

"Fish tacos," Coach Ken answered.

"For breakfast?"

"I eat them anytime and all the time," Coach Ken said. "Can't get enough of them ever since... ever since *The Day*."

"What's *The Day*?" Martin asked curiously.

"That's a story for another time," Coach Ken said as he got up from his desk and directed Martin to sit down in a chair, walked over, sat down next to him, and faced him. He looked at him with the stare of a focused prize fighter and said, "Martin, I'm not a man who minces words, so let me get right to the point. I asked you here for a reason, and it's because I have a few important questions to ask you. First I want to know how bad you want to make this team."

There was a pause. "Really bad. It means everything to me . . . and my family," he said as he nodded his head.

"Okay, that's good. Now I have an even more important question to ask you. How bad do you want to be great?"

Martin thought for a moment, but before he could answer, Coach Ken continued, "Because let me tell you something. Making the team is a goal. But striving for greatness is a life mission. There's a difference, and you have to be honest with yourself and you have to be honest with me. Don't rush the answer. I want you to really think about it."

Martin paused for what seemed like an eternity. He thought back to playing Pop Warner football, then travel ball and countless summer camps. Then high school and college . . . and then last night's game. From the first time he ever touched a football and put on his helmet and pads it was always the same feeling.

"Yes, Coach, I want to be great," he answered confidently. "It's all I've ever wanted. I've always wanted to be the best."

"Why?" coach asked.

"I don't know. There's always been something in me that has driven me. Honestly, at every level that I ever played, I was the best. I worked harder and loved the game more than anyone I knew."

"That's not surprising, and that's why I'm asking you these questions," Coach Ken responded. "But you have to remember that every guy here was the best player on his team. Everyone here had more talent than everyone he played against. But making it in this league requires more than talent. What got you to this level won't get you to the next. And that leads me to my final question. Are you willing to pay the price that greatness requires?"

Martin didn't hesitate. "Yes. I'll do whatever it takes."

"You sure about that?" Coach Ken asked as he cocked his head to the right and squinted his eyes. "I'm not looking for just words here. You see, everyone says they want to be great, but very few are willing to pay the price. When a player asks me how to get to the next level, I ask them how much they want it. Because if you want it you'll be willing to pay the price and invest the time, energy, sweat, and dedication that greatness requires. People think it's all about talent. But talent isn't enough anymore. Everyone here has talent. It's about infusing talent with heart, soul, spirit, and passion. It's about doing the things that make the best of the best better than everyone else. And these things have nothing to do with talent," he said, raising his voice as he smacked his hands together.

"So, if you tell me you are willing to pay the price and you really mean it, then I will work with you and do all I can to help you. As iron sharpens iron, I will mold you, develop you, train you, and teach to you to be the best of the best. But if you aren't willing to pay the price, then you just let me know. I will understand," he said lowering his voice. "I realize that not everyone is willing to pay the price, and that's okay. It's just that I'm not willing to waste my time on someone unless they want it as much as I want it for them. Life's too short. So I want you to think about it. I know you're probably a little shell shocked. Take the day and come to my office after practice and let me know what you decide. Be honest with yourself, Martin, and be honest with me."

"I will," answered Martin as he hobbled toward the door. He indeed was shell shocked, and he wasn't sure what hurt more, his ankle or his head. He didn't know Coach Ken had so much to say, especially to him, and he was surprised that he was willing to take the time to help him. "But before I leave, can I ask you a question?" Martin asked.

"Anything," answered Coach.

"Why me? Why do you want to help me?"

Coach stood up and gave Martin a big smile. "Three reasons, Martin. Number one, because I need a great running back that can make my linemen look good," he said with a hearty laugh.

"Number two, for reasons I'll tell you in due time.

"And number three, because you have *it*. We don't know what *it* is, but I know it when I see *it*. I've also found that *it* can be developed, sharpened, and strengthened, and I'm just the guy to help you do it. I'll see you later."

Chapter 8

On the Sideline

Martin spent a frustrating day standing and sitting on the sideline, watching practice instead of playing. He stood using his crutches until his arms got tired, and he sat on the bench until his butt hurt. He hated being injured, and he hated not playing football even more. When you were injured, the other players and coaches looked at you differently, and Martin didn't like it one bit. He stood there shaking his head, talking to himself. *I should be out there. How can I strive for greatness if I'm not on the field? And if I don't get better, then all the advice in the world from Coach Ken won't do any good.* He knew that the team had their third pre-season game coming up, and right after that the coaching staff would make their first cut. A bunch of guys would be let go from training camp and he didn't want to be one of them. Having Coach Ken in his corner was great, but he knew it would take a lot more than that to make the team—and getting healthy was going to be the biggest challenge.

Martin also had plenty of time to think about Coach Ken's questions, and being injured made him realize he wanted to play more than ever. He thought of his Momma, his fiancée, Shawna, who he missed terribly, and his family. He knew that he was trying to make the team for them. But playing the game of football was for him. He would do it even if no one paid him. He didn't want to be average. Life was too short to be average. He wanted to be great. He was willing to pay the price—any price.

As his ankle throbbed and his hand hurt from punching the bench he was sitting on, Martin felt more helpless than he had ever felt in his entire life. Mr. Control was no longer in control. There was nothing he could do to change his situation. He was stuck. All he could do was sit and wait. Wait for his ankle to heal. Wait to get back on the field. Wait to find out if he would make the team or not. And in that moment of helpless desperation, he slouched over and put his head in his hands and silently cried out, "Help me. Help me. Heal me. Heal me. I want to be well."

Chapter 9

The Playbook

 After practice Martin hobbled on his crutches to Coach Ken's office. He knocked on the door and walked in as Coach Ken was eating another fish taco.

"I'll have to get me one of those sometime," Martin said.

"You'll love 'em," Coach Ken responded. "The training camp chefs have certainly perfected them over the years. Took a while but they got it right.

"So how you doing, Martin?" Coach asked as he got up from this chair.

"To be honest, not very good, Coach. I'm not used to being injured and I'm not dealing with it very well. I got to get back on the field."

"You will," Coach Ken reassured him as he approached Martin.

"No, you don't understand—I've got to get on the field *now*," he said. "I thought a lot about what you said and my answer to your question is *yes*. I'm willing to pay the price. That's why I have to get better. After all, how I can I strive for greatness and work my tail off if I'm not on the field?"

Coach Ken shook his head and smiled as he put his large hand on Martin's shoulder. "You remind me a lot of the way I used to think. I thought that being great meant that I needed to get stronger, quicker, and faster. And while those things were certainly part of becoming a great football player, I have learned they are not where greatness begins.

"You see, striving for greatness doesn't start on the field. It starts right here, in your head. You win here first," he said, pointing to his forehead. "Then you win on the field."

"You sound like Gus," Martin said.

"Well, I'll take that as a compliment," Coach answered. "Gus and I have had many conversations about this over the years and he's been a wonderful student, friend, and teacher. He's more than an athletic trainer, you know. Everyone thinks he just deals with injuries and tapes ankles, but the guy could inspire a rock to move if the rock would listen. And the same things I have shared with Gus I want to share with you. Here, take this," Coach Ken said as he handed Martin a playbook.

Martin sighed and thought to himself, *Not another playbook*. His head hurt from memorizing the offense. He had never seen so many formations and different running plays. Plus he had to memorize the special teams playbook and the team rules and regulations playbook. Another playbook was the last thing he was interested in.

Coach Ken, sensing Martin's uneasiness, said, "Now, I know another playbook is the last thing you want to see, but this playbook is different. This playbook is like no other playbook you have ever seen. When I first got into coaching I made it my goal to help players become better. Since I had a lot of connections from my playing days, I traveled around the country and met with a lot of people who were considered the best in their fields of expertise. I met with coaches, athletes, CEOs, salespeople, musicians, artists, actors, teachers, bankers, and doctors. You name it, I met with them. I wanted to know what made the best better than everyone else, so I could help my players be their best. You know what I found, Martin?"

"What?" Martin asked without a clue where Coach Ken was going with this.

"I found that the best of the best all shared similar characteristics, principles, and habits. It didn't matter if they played football or the violin or they worked with numbers, a sledgehammer, or a scalpel—when I asked them how they approached their work and asked them to tell me about their routine and asked them why and how they had become the best, they would all say many of the same things. I honestly was a little disappointed at first. Like most people I was expecting a magic formula or some sort of secret recipe. I was hoping to hear something I hadn't heard before. But that didn't happen. Instead I received a valuable insight that there is a pattern to greatness that cuts across all ages, races, genders, and professions. There is a formula for success no matter what kind of work you do. There are things that the best do that others don't and things that they do better than everyone else. There is a way that the best of the best approach their life and work and craft that differentiates them from others. And this formula is predictable and simple to understand. But it's a process, and more than anything it requires someone who is willing to pay the price, which is why I needed to get that commitment from you, Martin. You understand what I'm telling you, right?"

Martin nodded as he looked at the playbook Coach had given him. On the cover it read:

Training Camp Playbook:
What the Best Do Better Than Everyone Else

"Yep, it's all in there," Coach added. "Everything I learned, all the wisdom that was shared with me, all the strategies, ideas, and principles that kept me awake at night are in this playbook. Over the years I've shared a copy of it with anyone who was willing to listen, learn, and do the work. Of course, I've tweaked it, refined it, and improved it, but the core ideas, strategies, and principles remain. And now I'll share it with you—if you are ready. You have to be ready, because once you start down this road, your life will never be the same. As I've told you before, greatness is a life mission."

"I'm ready," Martin answered, knowing that he liked what he heard so far. If there was a formula for success, he wanted to know it.

"Oh, and one more thing," Coach said, as he rested his chin on his fist. "I have to be straight up with you. I can't promise that this playbook will help you make the team. It's a process, after all, and it doesn't happen overnight. But I can promise you that if you commit to the principles I share with you and apply them to football or the work you do beyond football, you will rise to the top of your game in any initiative you pursue. So, you still up for this?" Coach asked, shrugging his shoulders and tightening his face. "If you don't want to go through with this, I completely understand."

Martin took a deep breath and paused for a long moment as he weighed the options. He certainly didn't want to work construction like his dad had done when Martin was a young boy. And the job he was offered by his college football coach's friend wasn't appealing. Football was his only option. There was nothing else he wanted to do. He decided to go for broke or fail trying. Being average wasn't an option for Martin Jones. He didn't know what the future held, but he did know that he wanted to be the best. "Yes, let's open the playbook," he said as he turned the cover to the first page.

Chapter 10

The Telescope

The first page featured a picture of a telescope. "What's with the telescope?" Martin asked.

"Look over there," Coach said pointing to the telescope by his window that faced toward the football field. "The telescope represents the big picture. It represents the greatness that the best strive for. I've found that the first and foremost trait of the best of the best is that *They know what they truly want,*" he said as he directed Martin to turn the page of the playbook, which looked like this:

 1. The Best know what they truly want.

"They know what they are working toward. It's often in the distance, but they have a clear picture of it in their mind and they can see it. Some formulate this vision because of a role model that inspired them and showed them that greatness was possible. Who was it for you?" he asked, knowing Martin had an answer.

"Walter Payton," Martin answered with a big smile on his face.

"Sweetness," coach responded as he paused and reflected for a moment. "They called him Sweetness because he ran with such style. What a football player. What a human being. We sure do miss him."

"He was one of the best," Martin said.

"Yes, he was, Martin, and that's what I'm talking about. For many who strive to be the best, there was a person before them who paved the way, who showed them that greatness was possible. Sometimes this person was a friend or mentor, and other cases it was a complete stranger who showed the world what being the best looked like.

"Now, for others who have become the best in their field of work, there was no role model for them. These people simply were given a God-inspired vision to pave the way and create something bold and new that had never been done before. They had a clear vision and they devoted their life to it."

"So they knew that they always wanted to be great at something?" Martin asked.

"Well, not exactly. Yes, there were some that always knew what they wanted, ever since they were young. But for many who became the best, they didn't always know what they wanted. They were just doing something they loved and didn't realize they were excelling. Then one day lightning struck and they had a 'Eureka!' moment where they thought, 'Hey, I can become great at this.'"

Coach continued, "Then there were those who were simply settling for mediocrity. They created a nice, average life with something they were average or good at, with a feeling in their gut that there is something more—something missing in their life—something that was left unsaid and undone. They wrote down goals because people said you need to do that, and yet the goals had nothing to do with what they truly wanted. They knew there was more, and thankfully one day they found it . . . or rather, I should say that their vision and purpose found them. Instead of being one of the sheep that followed the herd, they became shepherds who saw the way.

"But the common thread between all these stories and people is this: Regardless of when and how, whether by practical experience, role model, spiritual insight, or lightning strike, the best of the best all had a moment in their lives when their vision became clear. When they said, this is what I truly want, this is what I want to strive for and I will pay the price to make it happen. It was as if they looked through a telescope and saw their future. For some, it came when they were young. For others it was much later in life. But they all had that moment at some point when they had what I call a 'mountaintop experience.' I call it this because it's like they went to the mountaintop, pulled out a telescope, and saw their destination—the big-picture vision.

"Seeing it is important because to reach your destination you know you have to travel through the valley of hardship and struggle to get there. But your big-picture vision will fuel you during your journey and help you bear the struggle and overcome the hardship to reach your goal. When you know what you want and you see it, you will be willing to pay the price and overcome challenges to realize it."

"But what happens if someone doesn't know what they truly want?" Martin asked. "I have many friends who don't have a clue."

"If you don't know what you want, then you won't have a passion for it and you won't strive to be great at it. You'll be like 90 percent of the world's population who are either doing something they are good at or just collecting a paycheck. It's not truly what they want, so they don't pay the price to become great. Forget life mission. They're basically on life support just hoping to get through the day. Believe me. I know. That's where I was years ago after my football career was over.

"I decided to go into the restaurant business, and I was pretty good at it and the restaurants were successful. But one day after waking up feeling depressed I remember asking, 'Why am I not jumping out of bed? Why am I here? What do I truly want?' I realized I was happiest and most energized when I was around the game of football. The idea of coaching popped into my head and so I made a few calls, sold my restaurants, and started as an assistant to the assistant to the assistant, just to get my foot in the door. I was making basically nothing and yet I loved every minute of it. Sure, I was *good* at the restaurant business, but I am a *great* line coach. I think a lot of people spend their life being average or good at something but they don't strive to become great. That's no way to live, and that's why I've always told my four daughters, 'Don't choose your career based on what you think will please me. I don't care what you do. Just find something you love and are passionate about and pray for guidance that God will show you why you are here and reveal what you truly want. If you ask, you will receive. But whatever you do, don't be a 50 percenter. Invest 100 percent and every ounce of your energy in knowing what you want and becoming great at it. Strive to be your best and stand tall.' Even you, Martin, and your 5 feet, 7 inches can do this," Coach said with a big laugh.

Martin laughed and for a brief moment wondered what it would have been like growing up with a father. His dad had unfortunately died in a car accident on his way to a construction site one morning. His last memory of his father was having a football catch with him, but he was too young to remember any memorable advice his dad might have given him.

"So, how about you, Martin?" Coach Ken asked. "Do you see it? Do you have a vision of yourself playing in the NFL? Do you see what is possible? Do you see your future?"

"Yes, I see it, Coach," Martin said. "I saw it in college for the first time, and that's why I'm here. I remember when the thought first hit me, 'Hey, this dream really could happen.' And being here and after last night especially, I see it more now than ever. I could do this. I really could do it. Most importantly, I now also realize that I must pay the price to get it."

"Well, that's good to hear, because now that you know what you want, to be the best you must want it more than everyone else. The best of the best not only know what they want, but they want it more. They have a greater desire. That's the second trait in the playbook," Coach Ken said as he directed Martin to turn the page. The page looked like this:

 ## 2. The Best want it more.

"But how can you measure this desire?" Martin asked. "I mean, how can you compare two people and decide who wants it more? Who can judge that?"

"Ah, great question. You're smarter than your college coach said you were," Coach Ken said, laughing. "The answer is that we can't measure desire in terms of merely thought and wishes. After all, someone could wish for something twelve hours a day, but if they aren't taking initiative to make it happen, then what good is all the wanting? We must also measure desire in terms of actions, too.

"You see, I believe that everyone has a desire to be great. Everyone has a desire to accomplish something meaningful and have an impact. When I speak to teenagers I ask them if they want to be great. Of course they all say yes. Then I tell them that you want to be great because God made you to want to strive for greatness. But here's the difference. The best of the best are willing to do what it takes to *be* great. The best don't just think about their desire for greatness, they act on it. They have a high capacity for work. They do the things that others won't do, and they spend more time doing it. When everyone else is sleeping, the best are practicing and thinking and improving."

Martin couldn't help but think of the advice his momma would always give him. She would say that everyone is called by God to something and if you were called to be a bus driver, then you should develop your skills and become the best driver you could be. If you were called to be a teacher, then become the best teacher you can be. And if you were called to be football player, then you should become the best football player you can be. To settle for anything less than your best was a waste of the gifts and calling you have been given. It was selfish not to be your best, she would add, because as you developed and shared your gifts, the whole world benefited. *To deny being your best was to deny the gift you were meant to give others.* Perhaps that's why he worked so hard and perhaps that's why everything Coach Ken was telling him resonated with him.

"So, the best take action that demonstrates their greater desire," Martin asked. "That's the difference, right?"

"Well, yes and no," answered Coach Ken as he walked over to the telescope and pointed it toward the sky and directed Martin to take a look through it. "The best not only do the things that others won't do and invest the time others won't invest, but they also do so with passion and the intent to get better. The best are never satisfied with where they are. The third trait of the best is that they are always striving to get better."

3. The Best are always striving to get better.

"It's as if they look through the telescope pointed to the heavens and realize that there is a certain perfection, harmony, and beauty that exists, and everyone who has ever wanted to be great strives for this perfection—and when they get a glimpse of it in a golf swing, a basketball dunk, a home run, a soccer kick, a song, a dance, a painting, a sales pitch, a research project, a book, or a speech, they continue to pursue this perfection. They pursue it with passion as an internal fire of desire burns within them. And do you know what pursuing perfection requires, Martin?"

"Time and effort," he answered.

"Of course, those are essential, but what it really requires is a willingness to be uncomfortable. Here's the deal. If you are always striving to get better, then you are always growing. And if you are growing, then you are not comfortable. To be the best, you have to be willing to be uncomfortable and embrace it as a part of your growth process. It's a process, and I'm going to tell you how it works."

Chapter 11

Continuous Improvement

"The best are always looking for ways to learn, apply, improve, and grow. They are humble and hungry. They are lifelong learners," Coach continued.

"Did you know that when I was speaking in Dallas at a leadership conference, Zig Ziglar was in the front row, taking notes?"

"Who's Zig Ziglar?" Martin asked.

"Only one of the greatest motivational speakers of all time. He's 82 years old and he's taking notes, still trying to improve and grow. To me that's a lifelong learner. Too many people don't become great because they are not willing to learn and get better. They don't like being uncomfortable. They like the status quo. They like their comfort zone."

"What's wrong with being comfortable?" Martin asked.

"Everything," Coach answered. "Everything if you want to be the best. You are either getting better or worse but never staying the same. If you are not getting better, then it means you are getting worse. That's why the best are always pushing themselves out of their comfort zone as they strive to get better. Those who want to just be average and good are happy to be comfortable. But for the best, comfort is not an option. Take my four daughters, for example. One is a teacher, one is a doctor, one is a stay-at-home mom, and the other owns her own business. I sent them to the finest schools in the country. I spent a fortune on education. Told them I was frontloading them and setting them up for success; in case they married some dimwit, they would be able to take care of themselves."

Martin laughed as Coach Ken continued, "I also gave each one of them the Playbook and shared the lessons with them. All four of them will tell you that they are always asking themselves the questions, *How can I get better? How can I improve?* They have a burning desire to learn and grow. They are enjoying their lives, always striving to be their best, and thankfully they didn't marry any dimwits. They married some really good guys."

Martin laughed and nodded his head as Coach's words rang true to his heart. He always considered himself a life-long learner. He accepted advice from anyone who would give it and knew it always made him better. And now he was thankful that he was receiving some of the best advice in his life.

"So along these lines," Coach continued, "I need to ask you what you need to improve in your game."

Of course, Martin had a list already written in his head. "Well, let me see," he said with a big smile. "Blocking, pass receiving. Making quicker cuts once I get through the line of scrimmage. Not looking where I'm going to run before I get the ball, so the defense doesn't know where I'm going. Making better decisions on kickoffs and punt returns and about a hundred other things I'm working on."

"I like what I'm hearing," Coach said. "You know what you need to improve on to get better. That's big, Martin. Real big. You'd be surprised at how many people think they are all good and have no clue that they are playing at only 50 percent of their potential. There are hundreds of things that each one of us needs to do to get better, and the best are always looking for the one idea, technique, missing ingredient, new strategy that will make them even better.

"Even when people call them the best or say they are great, the best know they can do it even better and greater as they strive for perfection. The best see where there is room for improvement and their humility and passion drives them to improve. The average ones, however, don't see it or don't want to see it. They think that once they arrive at the door of greatness it will stay open forever, not realizing that if they don't improve the door will shut and in some cases will even fall on them. So in whatever you do, Martin, stay humble and hungry. Humble that you know you don't have all the answers, and you see everyone as a teacher. Hungry with a passion to improve and set new goals and milestones. Don't ever think you have arrived, because once you think you have arrived, you will start sliding back from where you came."

"I won't," Martin committed. "I always want to do it better."

Continuous Improvement

"That's great. You'd be just the guy, then, that Bill Walsh, one of the great football coaches of my time, would want on his team. Bill would often say that he feared success, not failure. He worried that once a player or team had success they would become complacent and stop striving to get better. He saw it too many times. A team would win a championship or a player would have a great season and then they would think that all they had to do was step on the field and they would automatically achieve the same results the following year, not realizing that it was the hard work, passion, and the constant striving to improve that resulted in success. I heard the same thing from the best in education, business, health care, science, entertainment, and other fields. Each year the best recommit themselves to new goals and being better than they were the year before. "The fact is that past success does not determine future success. Future success is the result of how you work and prepare and practice and how you strive to improve every day. It's a commitment that the best of the best make every week, every day, every hour, and every moment. Force yourself to be uncomfortable, Martin. Let it move you toward growth and action. Live and work with passion. Always strive to get better—and you will."

Chapter 12

The Benefits of a Coach

 After their conversation, Coach told Martin to head back to the training camp dorms, rest his ankle, and meet him in the weight room first thing in the morning, after receiving treatment from Gus.

So Martin hobbled out of Coach's office, alone with his thoughts and his injured ankle, and then made his way across the football field toward the housing complex and his room. As he reached the edge of the fields he turned back and looked at Coach Ken's window and saw the telescope facing the sky. He looked up and saw a clear sky and a full moon. It was a mild summer night and a cool breeze made it feel cooler than it was.

He thought about what Coach said about being uncomfortable and realized that there were many times in his football career when he was content and comfortable, but during those times a coach, a teacher, a friend of the family, his mother, or even a fan would push him to be better. He thought back to his sophomore year in college when the head coach and the running back coach would not stop yelling at him during training camp. He could do nothing right. Even when he made a great run they said he got tackled too easily. When he missed a block during pass protection they flat-out chided him in front of the entire team. Nothing was ever good enough. He told Shawna that he was going to quit, that he couldn't take it any more. But he stayed with it and once training camp was over his coaches acted like different people. They were encouraging and supportive and stopped yelling at him. He found out that they had planned it from the start. They felt he had become content with being good and needed to be pushed to be great.

Looking back, he realized that he wouldn't have become the player he was without their pushing and coaching. He realized that sometimes a person striving for greatness needs someone to push them out of their comfort zone. He realized that everyone needs a coach to help them strive to get better. Of course, not every coach should yell at their players. Some players don't respond well to yelling, even though it worked for him, he reasoned. Coaches need to treat each player differently based on what motivates the player.

And he realized that just as his coaches in college had pushed him to improve physically, Coach Ken was now pushing him to improve mentally. He reflected on what Coach Ken said about being the best, and he knew that being the best wasn't determined by where you were born or what school you went to or who your parents are. He knew success didn't care about these things and it didn't care about how great you were. It only cared about what you were doing today to strive to be the best and how hard you were willing to work and how much dedication you were willing to give and how much you could push yourself or allow yourself to be pushed.

He was thankful for his college coaches that they pushed him to this point and he was excited about what he was learning from Coach Ken. But that excitement turned to fear when he received another important phone call.

Martin answered the phone anxiously. "Hi Shawna, how's Momma? Is she alright?"

"She's doing okay. She tried to do too much, as usual. She's just tired. Not one of her best days, but don't worry."

"Don't worry," he yelled. "How can I not worry? I should come home right now."

"No, you shouldn't. You stay right where you are and you do what you are there to do. Do you understand me?" she said with a stern voice. "I got it covered and I'm taking good care of her. Besides, if you were here all your worrying would just make everyone nervous. So you just get better and use all that nervous energy on the field to do great. You got me, my big, strong NFL running back?"

"I got it," he said with a smile.

"Do you miss me?" she asked.

"Of course I miss you. I miss you like crazy," he answered, wishing he was able to see her right now. He knew his mother was right about her. She was definitely The One. She always told him *You know you've picked the right woman when she gives you strength,* and Shawna certainly did that.

"Well, that's all I need to know, Martin. And all you need to know is that I'll take good care of Momma. She'll be fine tomorrow. I'm making her take it easy. Now, do what you went there to do, Martin. I'll take care of everything else. Well, Momma wants me. I gotta go. Love you."

"Love you," Martin whispered as he arrived at his dorm room. Yes, Shawna was definitely The One. He walked in and not surprisingly his roommate wasn't there. Like many of the guys, he was out on the town having a good ol' time. But not Martin. Injury or no injury, that wasn't for him. He had his girl and he had football, and he didn't want anything to get in the way of his love and passion for both of them. He walked into his room, threw himself on the bed, turned on Sports Center, and tried to take his mind off his mother. With tears in his eyes, he fell asleep.

Chapter 13

The Myth

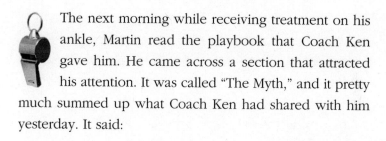 The next morning while receiving treatment on his ankle, Martin read the playbook that Coach Ken gave him. He came across a section that attracted his attention. It was called "The Myth," and it pretty much summed up what Coach Ken had shared with him yesterday. It said:

There is no such thing as an overnight success. Too many believe in the fantasy that superstar athletes, actors, musicians, doctors, pianists, Olympians, and others were born that way or simply stumbled on their success overnight. After all, the best of the best make what they do look so easy that people either think anyone can do it or that there are those who are chosen to do it. This myth is perpetuated by the media. On television we see the successful person performing his craft. We see the concert, the movie, the computer program, the presentation, the game, the play, the miracle surgery, the lecture, the Nobel Prize, the latest discovery, or the Olympic event. We see the end

result—the outcome—but what most of us don't see are the countless hours of sweat, toil, dedication, practice, and preparation that lead to greatness. The golf champion practiced thousands of puts before hitting the one to win the U.S. Open. The tennis champion hit a million backhands before winning Wimbledon. The rock star sang for countless hours before reaching stardom. The technology designer spent thousands of hours to create a new and revolutionary product that makes our lives easier. The teacher spent a career preparing and practicing ways to better connect with and teach her students before winning a teacher of the year award. The symphony practiced thousands of hours to create music that brought the audience to tears. And the sales team spent a year preparing for the important meeting that landed their biggest client. The ideal of the overnight success is a myth. Just as the Olympian must train for years for one defining race, you must wake up each day and practice, prepare, and train to be your best. Don't settle for mediocrity, but strive each day for excellence. It requires hard work, preparation, and hours of effort, but it's worth it.

Reading this was a good thing because Martin was about to learn what practice, preparation, and hard work were all about.

Chapter 14

The Game-Day Principle

 Martin walked into the weight room with a glimmer of hope that he would soon return to the football field. He even considered that maybe his mom's prayers were working. Gus said he was a really fast healer and gave him the go-ahead to walk on the ankle, although jogging and running were still out of the question. Martin looked across the room and saw Coach Ken standing by the bench press with Sully the strength coach. Sully was from Boston. He had played football for Cornell University and was an All-Ivy linebacker. Knowing he didn't have the speed to make it in the NFL, Sully pursued a career in physical therapy and eventually found his calling as a strength coach and performance expert. Sully and Coach Ken called for Martin to come meet them by the bench press.

"You working out today?" Sully asked.

"Well, I didn't think I could with my ankle," Martin answered.

"Nothing's wrong with your arms and chest," Sully said as he laughed with his Boston accent.

"No, my chest and arms are fine," Martin said knowing that Sully was indirectly calling him out.

"Great, then lay down on this bench press and put your legs on the bench so you don't put pressure on your ankle and let's bang out a few sets. We need to get your chest and triceps stronger so you can improve your pass blocking.

"You like the weight room?" Sully asked as Martin finished his first set.

"I do," answered Martin. "I practically lived in the weight room in college."

"Good," Sully said. "Because if you want to make it in this league, this weight room needs to be your second home. I watched you the other night and you are fast as lightning and you have an innate ability on the field, but that's not what's going to make you great. As Coach and I were discussing before you showed up, what will make you great is coming here every day, injured or not, and getting stronger every day. I've also got this agility and performance training program I need to share with you that's based on what Jerry Rice did all his years of playing. You know Jerry wasn't the fastest. And he wasn't the tallest. And over the years he wasn't the youngest. But Jerry worked and trained harder than any football player I've ever known. That's why he became the greatest wide receiver to ever play the game. Everyone thinks he was the best because of how he performed on Game Day, *but actually it's how he prepared for Game Day that made him perform so well.* So if you want to be great you have to commit to a challenging process of preparation."

"He's right," Coach Ken added. "Yesterday I told you that you had to be willing to pay the price. Well, that price is paid with countless hours of hard work on the field and off the field. In fact, most of our time is actually spent preparing off the field, and it's not always fun. It's the same way with every aspect of life. I call it the Game-Day Principle. Five percent of a person's life is made up of our performance on game day, while 95 percent is made up of the time we are preparing, practicing, and waiting to perform. Think about it: We spend two hours on the field each day for practice and three hours, tops, during game day, and yet we spend thousands of hours in the weight room, training in the off-season, conditioning during the week, studying film, memorizing playbooks, the list goes on. The fact is, how we practice and prepare with 95 percent of our time determines how we perform on game day. It requires thousands of hours of practice, dedication, hard work, and focus."

"I know," answered Martin. "I read the part about 'The Myth' in the playbook. I never thought of success like that, and it made a lot of sense when I looked at what it has taken me to be here today."

"Good," answered Coach Ken. "Because it's going to take you even more to get to where you are going."

Martin nodded and smiled as Sully nodded his head and added, "Yes, the Myth. I love that part. So true. It reminds me of what Ben Hogan said when he was asked about playing great golf. He said, 'It's in the dirt.' Everyone thinks greatness is sexy, but it's dirty—hard work."

As Coach Ken, Sully, and Martin continued talking, Martin soaked up everything they said, knowing he had the desire and willingness to pay the price. But what he didn't know was that the difference between the best and the rest was very small.

Chapter 15

Ten Percent Better

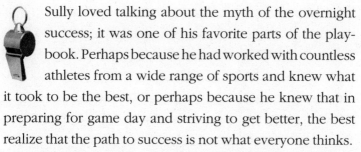 Sully loved talking about the myth of the overnight success; it was one of his favorite parts of the playbook. Perhaps because he had worked with countless athletes from a wide range of sports and knew what it took to be the best, or perhaps because he knew that in preparing for game day and striving to get better, the best realize that the path to success is not what everyone thinks.

Sully held up his coffee cup and showed Martin. "I have a friend who's an executive at Starbucks. So one day we're talking and I ask him what makes Starbucks so great. I'm expecting him to tell me it's the coffee. But he tells me that it's the fact that they do a hundred things 10 percent better than everyone else. And so I'm saying to myself that this is no different than football or baseball." He turned to Martin. "Do you know the difference between a .250 batter and a .350 batter?"

"I'm guessing it's more than 100 points," Martin said.

"Yes, it's more than a 100 points," Sully said. "A lot more. It's the difference between a Hall of Fame baseball player and an average player. It's the difference between millions of dollars of salary and endorsements. It's the difference between fame and fortune. Yet if you calculate 162 games a year, 4 or 5 bats a game, the difference between a .250 batter and a .350 batter is only 1.7 hits a week. It's the little things that separate the best from the rest. In striving to get better and working hard every day, the best realize that success is not about the big things. Success is all about the little things."

"Great stuff," Coach Ken said as he patted Sully on the back. "I love that baseball analogy because everyone thinks that being the best is about the touchdown, the home run, the dunk, the blistering tennis serve, or the hole in one, but it's really about doing all the little things over time 10 percent, 5 percent, or even 1 percent better than everyone else. Interestingly enough, for all their greatness, the best aren't that much better than the others. They are simply a little better at a lot of things. Everyone thinks that success is complicated, but it's really simple. In fact, the best don't do anything different. They just do the ordinary things better. This is number four in the playbook, and it was inspired by Chuck Noll, the great Pittsburgh Steelers coach who won four Super Bowls."

 4. The Best do ordinary things better than everyone else.

"But how do they do the ordinary things better?" Martin asked.

"By practicing and practicing, focusing and improving every day on the little things," Coach answered.

"It's like I tell my wife who loves tennis," Sully added. "Just keep practicing and doing those ball drills every week and you'll improve. And I say the same thing to my daughter, who is playing the piano. One day of practice isn't much. But if you practice every day, over the course of a year you'll get really good. And over the course of a number of years, you'll be amazing. In fact, I read recently in a great book, *Outliers*, by Malcolm Gladwell, that there was a study done in the 1990s by psychologist K. Anders Ericsson and two colleagues at Berlin's elite Academy of Music. They found that what separated the best violinists from the good and average performers was not talent but rather the amount of time they practiced throughout their life. By the age of 20, the best performers had practiced for a total of 10,000 hours, the good performers practiced for 8,000 hours, and the average performers practiced for only 4,000 hours. The only difference was the amount of practice. It's not rocket science. There's simply no substitute for practice and hard work."

The coaches were silent as Martin finished his bench-press set and took a deep breath. Certainly hard work and practice were themes that seemed to keep coming up. He realized that no one would be the best without them. But what Martin didn't realize was that being the best was not just practicing, but the right kind of practice. It wasn't just about working hard, but working hard on the right things. This would be the next lesson he would learn from Coach Ken and Sully.

Chapter 16

The Microscope

 Coach Ken turned to Sully and asked him to open the playbook and show Martin the page with the microscope on it. "Hey, Sully, you remember how to open a book, right?" he asked jokingly. "After all, you were an Ivy League student once."

Sully laughed and said, "Yeah, I remember," as he showed Martin the microscope.

Coach then turned his attention to Martin. "We talked about the telescope representing the big-picture vision for your future. It's the perfection and greatness that you strive for. Well, the microscope represents the zoom-focused actions you need to take each day to realize the vision you see through the telescope. As Edison said, '*Vision without execution is hallucination.*'"

Everyone laughed.

"The microscope is all about execution, and to execute with excellence you must take zoom-focused actions. *Zoom-focus* means that you are not just working hard, but working hard on the right things. It means you must identify the key 'little ordinary things' that are fundamental to

61

your success, and then you must focus on them, practice them, and strive to execute them to perfection. The best zoom-focus, and this is the fifth trait of what the best do better than everyone else."

 ## 5. The Best zoom-focus.

"For example," Coach Ken continued, "did you know that John Wooden, the legendary UCLA basketball coach, would teach his players how to tie their shoes on the first day of practice?"

"Why would he do that?" Martin asked.

"Because he knew that a player couldn't run or jump or play at their best if their shoes weren't tied. Success is all about the fundamentals. And the fundamentals are little and ordinary and often boring. But to be the best, I'm telling you now, you must master them. You must become a master of the ordinary. In every act of greatness, whether in sports, business, science, or the arts, the best of the best accomplish extraordinary feats by doing ordinary things with extraordinary consistency, commitment, and focus. As in baseball, you must decide what will help you get 1.7 hits more per week. You must decide what fundamentals require your zoom focus. In football the fundamentals vary by position. In life they vary by the work you do and the job you have. Every job, whether you are carrying a football, a briefcase, a musical instrument, a computer, or a shovel, features fundamentals that can be mastered, and if you master them you will become the best at what you do. This is what I teach and drill into my linemen every day, and it's why they are the best in the league."

"And know this," Sully said, joining the conversation. "It doesn't happen overnight. Some call it the 10-year rule, which says that it takes 10 years of practice to become great at something. Others call it the 10,000 hour rule, which says you must practice something for 10,000 hours to master it. But however long it takes, I call it the *practice till you master the fundamentals* rule."

"That's why greatness is a life mission," Coach Ken said. "It's not just about striving to get better, it's about getting better by focusing on the right things. It's not just about practice, but *focused* practice. It's not just about taking action, but taking *zoom-focused* action. It's about practicing and perfecting the fundamentals."

"I couldn't agree more," Sully added. "You know, I always get a good laugh when announcers after a football game will ask a Coach why they won and you can always tell they are expecting some deep answer. The coach will often say, 'Well, we ran the ball well. We blocked well. We tackled well. We threw the ball well.' The announcer is looking for more, but there really isn't anything more. The recipe for success is not complicated. The art is in staying focused and being able to put the recipe together. It's about practice and execution."

"It's the same way in business," Coach Ken said. "When I interviewed some of the top sales guys for a company to find out why they were the best, I didn't hear any secret recipe. They simply said that they planned their day. They made their calls. They followed up. They did this day in and day out. They committed to the process of focusing on the fundamentals for their business, and it made all the difference.

"The key is to focus on improving each day and to take the necessary action steps. If you incrementally improve each day, each week, each month, each quarter, by the end of the year you'll see remarkable results and growth. When you zoom-focus on the process, the outcome takes care of itself. Great coaches, great teams, great players, and the best at what they do are able to zoom-focus, to create a system and process to master the fundamentals. This system and process drive the way they think, their practice and preparation, and how they approach each day. Over time, by committing to this process and system, the best develop their skill and enhance their performance as they strive for excellence and perfect execution. And that's why I always say that championships are not won on Super Bowl Sunday. They are won in training camp. They are won by how we practice and prepare throughout the season in August, September, October, and November. They are won by zoom-focusing and committing to the process.

Martin couldn't help but think about his own career and process over the years. He approached the game with such intensity and drive and was always trying to figure out how to get the edge. Yet he realized that maybe in this drive to get the edge and find the latest performance strategy, maybe he had ignored an important fundamental crucial to success. He wondered what else he needed to zoom-focus on to take his game to the next level. What had he not considered? What had he ignored? The answers would be key to the success of anyone striving to be the best.

Chapter 17

Mental Zoom-Focus

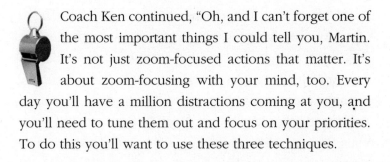 Coach Ken continued, "Oh, and I can't forget one of the most important things I could tell you, Martin. It's not just zoom-focused actions that matter. It's about zoom-focusing with your mind, too. Every day you'll have a million distractions coming at you, and you'll need to tune them out and focus on your priorities. To do this you'll want to use these three techniques.

1. "First, *ask one question*. Each day when you wake up in the morning ask the question, 'What are the three most important things I need to do today that will help me create the success I desire?' Then each day take action on those three things.

2. "Second, *say no and yes*. My friend once told me, 'If the devil can't make you bad, he'll make you busy.' He reminded me that we need to stop scattering our energy and wasting our time on trivial things that have nothing to do with our vision and goals and start saying yes to our priorities and to what truly matters. Each day we must make choices, and

those choices include saying *no* to some people and opportunities so that we can say *yes* to the greater work we are meant to do.

3. "Third, *tune out distractions.* Don't listen to what others say about you. After all, we don't talk this game, we play it. Tune out the distractions and zoom-focus on what you need to do every day to be your best. Do your talking on the field. Don't compare yourself to others. Don't look at the depth chart. Don't listen to the naysayers. Every day, focus on continuous improvement and getting better.

"And the last piece of advice about being mentally zoom-focused is something that we'll talk about after practice. Right now I have to get ready and you need to finish your workout. I'll see you in my office later," he said as he pointed to Martin and then patted Sully on the back and thanked him for his valuable insights. And as Coach Ken walked toward the exit across the room, he turned back toward Martin and shouted, "It's about mental toughness. Mental toughness is everything."

Chapter 18

Patience

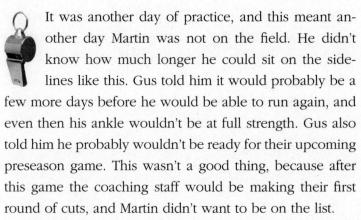 It was another day of practice, and this meant another day Martin was not on the field. He didn't know how much longer he could sit on the sidelines like this. Gus told him it would probably be a few more days before he would be able to run again, and even then his ankle wouldn't be at full strength. Gus also told him he probably wouldn't be ready for their upcoming preseason game. This wasn't a good thing, because after this game the coaching staff would be making their first round of cuts, and Martin didn't want to be on the list.

It had been only a few days since his two-touchdown performance but the media's excitement over Martin Jones was already gone. They had moved on to covering other star players who were healthy and able to practice. Martin knew that's how it went. When you were on the field and playing great, everyone wanted a piece of you. When you were injured, it was as if you were a ghost. Even the other players and coaches barely talked to him. After all, they were focused on preparing for practice and winning games. They were getting ready to go to battle. They didn't have time to deal with the walking wounded. That was the trainer's job.

Martin accepted all this, but he still didn't like it. And as Martin was feeling sorry for himself, one of the veterans who was the star running back on the team came over to him during the water break, smiled, and told him to keep his head up and that he'll be healthy in no time. The short exchange only lasted a few seconds, but it lifted Martin's spirits. Someone besides Coach Ken actually talked to him. It wasn't much, but it meant everything, and it was just what Martin needed to keep himself sane and hopeful about the future. Coach Ken had said that it's about mental toughness before he left the weight room, but unfortunately Martin was feeling pretty weak about his situation. Hopefully Coach Ken would have some answers after practice.

Chapter 19

Mental Toughness

Martin walked slowly to Coach Ken's office after a long and frustrating day on the sidelines. His ankle was sore but he was not about to continue using crutches. He knocked on the door and no one answered. When he walked in, Coach Ken was sitting at his desk taking the last bite of his fish taco.

"Let me guess: fish taco for dinner," Martin said, smiling.

"All the time. Breakfast, lunch, or dinner. Fish is great brain food and good for mental toughness, believe it or not," Coach said as he walked over to Martin and put his hand on his shoulder. He added, "As I told you earlier, mental toughness is the key. The brain is an interesting thing. It can actually be molded and impacted by the foods we feed it and the thoughts we feed it. A lot of people think that mental toughness is something we are born with. And while genes do play a part, the research shows that it's something we can develop. I have a friend who is a pro golfer, and he's gone head to head with Tiger Woods. He told me that everyone focuses on Tiger's swing and training program. They try to emulate what he is doing physically. But what they should be doing is following his mental routine and attempting to develop the same type of mental focus and strength. That's where Tiger wins every time. The thing is, Tiger's been doing it for years. He wasn't born a tiger. He became a tiger by developing mental toughness from an early age, and that's what I want to talk to you about today. To be the best you have to train and develop your mind as much as your body, and you must start *now*."

"Gus told me that the other day," Martin said.

"Well, good. Gus and I make a great team because now I'm going to tell you how to do it. Just as you build physical muscle by lifting weights, you can build mental muscle by doing exercises like positive self-talk, visualization, breathing, meditation, and prayer each day. Mental muscle is essential because in all my research and conversations I found that the sixth trait of the best of the best, regardless of profession or area of expertise, is that that they are mentally stronger." Coach then directed Martin to turn the playbook to the page titled "Mental Toughness." It said:

 6. The Best are mentally stronger.

"And the great news," Coach continued, "is that if you are already mentally strong, you can become stronger, and if you are not mentally strong now, you can build mental and emotional muscle starting today."

"Good," said Martin, "because this injury has gotten me feeling mentally weak and emotionally drained. I've never been injured like this, and it's driving me crazy."

"Well, that's just the point I'm making," Coach countered. "Being mentally strong means you are able to overcome these kinds of situations. It means you stay positive through adversity. It means you are resilient when facing pressure, challenges, and change."

Martin knew this all to well. After all, he had grown up with a mother whose name was Joy and who always talked about having a positive attitude and sharing positive energy. She would tell Martin not to let "energy vampires" get him down. She had driven a bus for years until her heart problems forced her to take a leave of absence. She had to deal with all sorts of negative people and situations, yet she always seemed to turn people and their situations around. She was an inspiration to Martin, and thinking about her made him feel guilty for being so negative about an ankle injury when his mother was dealing with far worse problems, and yet she was far more positive and optimistic than he was.

"You know, all that you are saying about being mentally tough reminds me of my mother," he said. "She always talked to me about playing with positive energy and staying positive."

"Well, your mother is a smart woman," Coach said. "Becoming the best is a process. It's a long and difficult process and it takes loads and loads of positive energy. First and foremost, you'll need to stay positive and focused during all those hours of practice that greatness requires. There will be days you don't want to practice. There will be times when you just don't feel it. That's when your mental strength kicks in and you do what it takes and you pay the price. You do so because you are more committed and mentally stronger.

"You'll also need to be mentally tough because as you strive to be the best you'll face many distractions and pressure from the outside world and negative noise from your own self-doubt. It's a process that will test who you are and what you truly want. Mental toughness is a big part of the answer.

"Today's world is no longer a sprint or a marathon. It's a series of sprints combined with a boxing match. You're not just running, you are getting hit along the way. You're getting hit by life. You're getting hit on the field. You're getting hit by the critics and doubters and even at times by the people closest to you. And the best are able to respond and overcome all of this with mental and emotional toughness. You know exactly what I'm talking about, don't you, Martin."

Martin nodded. He felt like an expert in dealing with adversity. Every time the naysayers would come out of the woodwork, his mother would always tell him to let them talk while he did his talking on the field. And she would say that if you were right with God, all the negativity in the world couldn't penetrate your spiritual armor. She told him that this was his foundation and if he had it, he had the strength to take on anything. And as he thought about his mother he realized his foundation wasn't very strong now. It had been cracked by all the hits he and his mother had taken lately. He knew all too well what it was like to get hit on and off the field. He just hoped he had the strength to fight through it.

"It's no secret," Coach continued. "You have to be mentally and emotionally stronger than your challenges, your detractors, and your situation. You have to be able to tune out the negative noise from the outside and turn off the negative thoughts on the inside. You have to stay calm, focused, and energized on game day and learn how to tune out the distractions during the week. When everyone tells you that you are great, you don't let it go to your head; when they say you stink, you don't let it go to your head."

"So true," Martin said as he laughed.

"But here's the thing. Mental toughness doesn't happen by osmosis. Like everything, it is a process, and as I said earlier, it can be developed. And to help you do this I created a technique called *weed and feed.*"

"Isn't that for yards and grass?" Martin asked.

"Yes, it is. And it's also for our minds, because our minds are like a garden. Each day you need to weed out the negativity and feed it positivity. You need to weed the self-doubt and negative talk and feed it positive thoughts, memories, visuals, and prayer."

"How do I do this?" Martin asked, knowing his mind needed a lot of weeding lately.

"Simple," Coach answered. "Each day you think of your mind as a garden and you pay attention to your thoughts. You know that if you don't weed out the negative thoughts, then they will take over your mind. You also know that if you continuously plant positive thoughts, eventually the weeds of negativity will have nowhere to breed and grow. It's a process and it works. Just as you practice running, blocking, and catching, you must practice thinking positive thoughts and eliminating negative thoughts. You realize that being positive or negative is a habit, and you choose the positive."

"I know what I'm going to choose from now on," Martin said as he walked over to the window and looked at the telescope and the microscope. He felt different. He wasn't sure how. He just felt different. He realized Gus was right. Sometimes an injury is a good thing. It was as if time had slowed down, and with Coach Ken's advice he was able to approach everything a little differently. He felt more aware, more clear, and more mentally prepared. Coach Ken's words gave him a much needed boost. He was eager to learn more, so it was a good thing that before he left their meeting Coach Ken encouraged him to read the playbook that night. Coach Ken told him to focus on the "Twenty Ways to Get Mentally Tough" section.

Twenty Ways to Get Mentally Tough

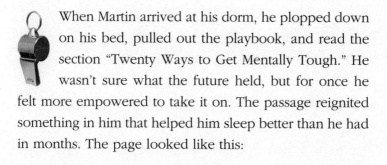

When Martin arrived at his dorm, he plopped down on his bed, pulled out the playbook, and read the section "Twenty Ways to Get Mentally Tough." He wasn't sure what the future held, but for once he felt more empowered to take it on. The passage reignited something in him that helped him sleep better than he had in months. The page looked like this:

1. When you face a setback, think of it as a defining moment that will lead to a future accomplishment.
2. When you encounter adversity, remember, the best don't just face adversity; they embrace it, knowing it's not a dead end, but a detour to something greater and better.
3. When you face negative people, know that the key to life is to stay positive in the face of negativity, not in the absence of it. After all, everyone will have to overcome negativity to define themselves and create their success.

4. When you face the naysayers, remember the people who believed in you and spoke positive words to you.

5. When you face critics, remember to tune them out and focus only on being the best you can be.

6. When you wake up in the morning, take a morning walk of gratitude and prayer. It will create a fertile mind ready for success.

7. When you fear, trust. Let your faith be greater than your doubt.

8. When you fail, find the lesson in it, and then recall a time when you have succeeded.

9. When you head into battle, visualize success.

10. When you are thinking about the past or worrying about the future, instead focus your energy on the present moment. The *now* is where your power is the greatest.

11. When you want to complain, instead identify a solution.

12. When your own self-doubt crowds your mind, weed it and replace it with positive thoughts and positive self-talk.

13. When you feel distracted, focus on your breathing, observe your surroundings, clear your mind, and get into The Zone. The Zone is not a random event. It can be created.

14. When you feel all is impossible, know that with God all things are possible.

15. When you feel alone, think of all the people who have helped you along the way and who love and support you now.
16. When you feel lost, pray for guidance.
17. When you are tired and drained, remember to never, never, never give up. Finish strong in everything you do.
18. When you feel like you can't do it, know that you can do all things through Him who gives you strength.
19. When you feel like your situation is beyond your control, pray and surrender. Focus on what you can control and let go of what you can't.
20. When you're in a high-pressure situation and the game is on the line, and everyone is watching you, remember to smile, have fun, and enjoy it. Life is short; you only live once. You have nothing to lose. Seize the moment.

Chapter 21

A Bad Day

 Everyone has bad days, and unfortunately there was nothing Martin could do to avoid this one. Ironically, it followed a night when Martin made a commitment to be mentally tough and choose the positive. But as so often happens, a desire to make a positive change is met with a series of immediate challenges and setbacks, as though the enemy knows you are putting on the armor and decides to attack you before you are powerful and ready. Unfortunately, Martin was vulnerable and susceptible to attack.

Martin arrived at the treatment room only to receive the news from Gus that he wasn't on the active list for the third preseason game in a few days. This meant even if his ankle improved he still wouldn't be able to play. "Look at the bright side," Gus said, "at least now you have a few more good days to rest and heal your ankle."

"Bright side? What bright side?" Martin thought as he considered the strong possibility that there might not be a next week for him. Unfortunately, Martin wasn't staying positive.

The news got worse when Martin went to see Coach Ken and he confirmed that he was indeed on the inactive list. When Martin asked Coach if this meant he would be cut next week, Coach Ken said he honestly couldn't say one way or another. It wasn't up to him. It was up to the big man (the head coach). To make matters even worse, Coach Ken told Martin he didn't have time to meet over the next few days because he would have to focus and prepare for the game.

"But don't worry," he said. "Everything will work out the way it's supposed to. Just focus on those twenty tips to get mentally tough over the next few days and we'll meet again the day after the game. The best is yet to come, and I'm planning for you to still be here next week. You have to stay positive. Just like we talked about, Martin, mental toughness is key."

Unfortunately Martin didn't share his optimism—and he had good reason. One of the other rookies vying for a spot on the team was doing amazing things in practice and at this moment he was higher on the depth chart than Martin. If someone was going to get cut it would be Martin.

Martin went back into the treatment room after everyone headed onto the field for practice, and found Gus, who was still in his office finishing paperwork.

"Gus, is there anything, I mean anything, we can do to get my ankle healed more quickly?"

"There's no rush," Gus said. "You're inactive for the game regardless."

"I know," Martin said, "but if by chance I don't get cut, I've got to be ready to go first thing next week. Is there anything else we can do to speed the healing up? Hyperbaric chamber? Sound waves? Rain dance? Anything?"

"Well, there is one thing. It's this guy I know. Strange but gifted. He's got a gift. Works on all sorts of famous musicians, celebrities, and a few open-minded athletes."

"Sounds like my guy," Martin said. "If there's one thing I am that's open-minded about getting healthy."

"Okay, I'll make sure he's here for treatment tomorrow morning and we'll see what we can do," Gus said.

"Thanks, Gus," Martin said. "Finally, some type of good news," he thought. For a moment he felt hopeful. But why, he had no idea.

A Bad Day

Chapter 22

Heal Strong

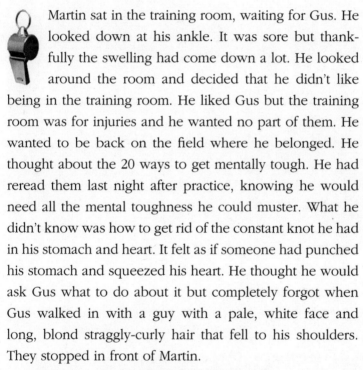 Martin sat in the training room, waiting for Gus. He looked down at his ankle. It was sore but thankfully the swelling had come down a lot. He looked around the room and decided that he didn't like being in the training room. He liked Gus but the training room was for injuries and he wanted no part of them. He wanted to be back on the field where he belonged. He thought about the 20 ways to get mentally tough. He had reread them last night after practice, knowing he would need all the mental toughness he could muster. What he didn't know was how to get rid of the constant knot he had in his stomach and heart. It felt as if someone had punched his stomach and squeezed his heart. He thought he would ask Gus what to do about it but completely forgot when Gus walked in with a guy with a pale, white face and long, blond straggly-curly hair that fell to his shoulders. They stopped in front of Martin.

"Martin, I'd like you to meet my friend Don. He's the guy I told you about yesterday," Gus said.

"How ya doing," Martin said as he looked at Don. "Thank you for coming."

"Well, don't thank me yet. I haven't done anything," Don said as he looked at Martin with his big, wide, piercing eyes.

Martin didn't know what to expect.

"So which ankle is it?" Don asked.

"Right here," Martin said as he pointed to it.

"Ah yes," Don said as he put his hands on the ankle and looked up to the ceiling.

"What do you think?" Martin asked nervously.

"I think we can make it better."

"How?"

Don put his finger to his mouth as though to say *shhhhsh*.

Then he grabbed Martin's ankle in his hands and started to maneuver it.

"Aoooowwwww," Martin squealed uncomfortably.

"He's a loud one," Don said in a quite calm voice to Gus.

"Have you ever heard of acupuncture?" Don asked Martin, trying to calm him down.

Martin nodded in pain.

"Well, acupuncture is all about stimulating the energy, or *chi*, in the body, to create energy flow. The body is made of energy. Everyone knows that. It's in all the science books and everything. We look physical, but at the core we're all energy. A healthy body is like a river that is flowing. An injured body is like a river that is dammed up. Injuries stop energy flow. I create energy flow so the body can heal more quickly. Acupuncture creates a trickle of energy flow. Me, I create the gush. I open up the dam."

"How do you do it?" Martin asked as he watched Don massage the back of his calf down to his Achilles' heel.

"Years of studying the anatomical structure of the body," he said. "Years of living in Asia. And years of practice. It's also a gift. I'm a conduit for the power. See this," Don said as squeezed Martin's calf. "This is your problem. Tightness here caused your ankle to weaken and buckle. Everything in the body is connected. You need to keep it healthy, aligned, and flowing."

Don continued squeezing and touching different parts of the ankle and calf as Martin winced in pain. "Don't worry, it hurts now but it will feel better later. And tomorrow you'll have a new and improved ankle," Don said as he closed his eyes and continued his work.

"What do you mean that you're a conduit for the power?" Martin asked, concerned that Don was a little off his rocker.

"The power that flows through everything," Don said, as if Martin should know this. "I don't do the healing. I'm just the conduit. That's my gift. I allow the power to flow through me."

"How?" Martin asked. He was now very curious.

"Philippians 4:13," Don said as he finished working on Martin's ankle. "Well, you're good to go. You're going to love the way you feel tomorrow," he said as he looked intensely into Martin's eyes, reached into his pocket, and handed him a bracelet that said "Heal Strong" on it. "Wear this and pray that your ankle will be stronger tomorrow than it was before the injury. Until next time," he said, acknowledging Gus, and then he walked out the door.

Martin and Gus looked at each other. "Like I said, strange but gifted," Gus whispered.

"You got that right," Martin responded as he put the bracelet on next to the one his mother had given him. He only hoped that Don in all his strangeness was right about his feeling great tomorrow.

Chapter 23

Feeling Better

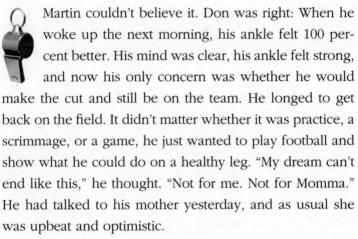Martin couldn't believe it. Don was right: When he woke up the next morning, his ankle felt 100 percent better. His mind was clear, his ankle felt strong, and now his only concern was whether he would make the cut and still be on the team. He longed to get back on the field. It didn't matter whether it was practice, a scrimmage, or a game, he just wanted to play football and show what he could do on a healthy leg. "My dream can't end like this," he thought. "Not for me. Not for Momma." He had talked to his mother yesterday, and as usual she was upbeat and optimistic.

"The doctors say that my condition has stabilized," she said. "It's not getting worse and it's not getting better. But they can't guarantee it will stay this way. At any moment it could collapse, they warned me. But it's like I tell everyone. God has pressed the pause button. Nothing bad is going to happen. I'm going to be fine. I have my faith."

"That's great, Momma," Martin said, knowing he didn't share her confidence.

"That's right, my baby boy. I have enough for both of us."

And as Martin thought about their conversation, he just smiled. She always told Martin that he was her heart and that she loved him more than life itself. She picked him up when he fell down. She encouraged him when he failed. She gave him the strength and the confidence to go for his dream. When others said he couldn't do it, she told him he could. When his father died, she took on his role in addition to hers. She worked hard, went to church, took care of her family, and never missed one of his football games in high school or college. She was the loudest fan in the stadium, and he always heard her cheers. Martin realized that he wasn't her heart. She was his. She was his source of strength. And now that source of strength was sick and in need of help. The one who was always there for him now needed him. The one he always turned to couldn't help. Martin wanted desperately to be able to help save her, but unfortunately the situation was beyond his control, and it drove him crazy. The only thing he could do was try to get healthy and get back on the football field.

Chapter 24

Preparation

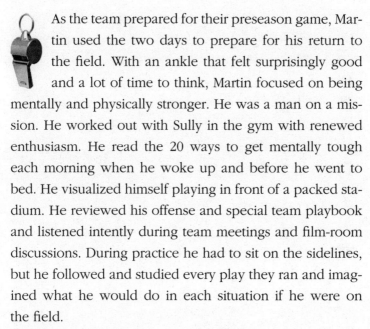 As the team prepared for their preseason game, Martin used the two days to prepare for his return to the field. With an ankle that felt surprisingly good and a lot of time to think, Martin focused on being mentally and physically stronger. He was a man on a mission. He worked out with Sully in the gym with renewed enthusiasm. He read the 20 ways to get mentally tough each morning when he woke up and before he went to bed. He visualized himself playing in front of a packed stadium. He reviewed his offense and special team playbook and listened intently during team meetings and film-room discussions. During practice he had to sit on the sidelines, but he followed and studied every play they ran and imagined what he would do in each situation if he were on the field.

And even though most of his teammates ignored him, the injured nobody, he cheered them on and encouraged them when they made a great play—even the other rookie who might make the team instead of him. He figured that no one could possibly know his situation, and for all he knew other players were dealing with their own challenges as well. Each player wanted to make the team as much as he did, and Martin, always the leader, shared the positive energy with anyone who would receive it. He wanted his team to do well. He also wanted just one more shot for himself. Just one shot to show that he had what it took to make it in the big time. After tomorrow night's game, he would know whether this shot would be granted.

Chapter 25

The Cut

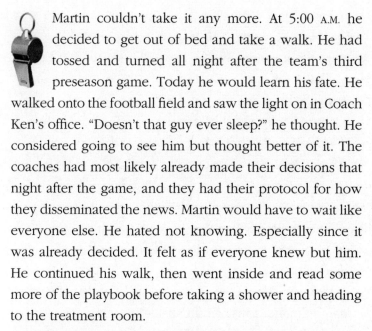Martin couldn't take it any more. At 5:00 A.M. he decided to get out of bed and take a walk. He had tossed and turned all night after the team's third preseason game. Today he would learn his fate. He walked onto the football field and saw the light on in Coach Ken's office. "Doesn't that guy ever sleep?" he thought. He considered going to see him but thought better of it. The coaches had most likely already made their decisions that night after the game, and they had their protocol for how they disseminated the news. Martin would have to wait like everyone else. He hated not knowing. Especially since it was already decided. It felt as if everyone knew but him. He continued his walk, then went inside and read some more of the playbook before taking a shower and heading to the treatment room.

When he arrived at the treatment room he interacted with the trainers and Gus, hoping they would give away a clue or something regarding his fate, but they said nothing. They treated his ankle and wished him luck. Perhaps they didn't know. Then, while he was about to head to the weight room to get a workout in, his running-back coach grabbed him and said the head coach wanted to see him in his office.

When they arrived, the head coach directed Martin and his running-back coach to have a seat. Martin's heart started pounding to the point it felt like it was going to come out of his chest. This was the end of the line, and Martin prepared himself for the worst. The head coach said, "I like what I saw from our running backs last night, Martin, but I really like what I saw from you last game. How's your ankle?" coach asked.

"Great," Martin said. "I'm ready to go. All healed up."

"Good," said Coach, "Because we're going to give you another week to see what you've got. I have to be honest with you, Martin. You're going to have to really show us more of what you showed us the other night if you're going to make this team. And you have to stay healthy. I don't want to give a roster spot to someone who's going to be injured all year."

"You won't have to worry about that," Martin said, jumping up and down on the inside.

"Excellent," coach said. "Well, as you know, today's a light day with no pads, and tomorrow begins more of the fun. So get ready to show us what you've got this week and we'll give you plenty of playing time this last preseason game. Then we'll both know if you're ready to play in this league."

"Thanks for the opportunity," Martin said as he walked toward the door. When he got outside he thanked and high-fived his running-back coach and ran to Coach Ken's office to talk about the news.

Chapter 26

Faith

Martin walked into Coach Ken's office. He was so excited he didn't knock.

"I just got the news from Coach," he said.

"I'm really happy for you, Martin. I pushed for you. All the coaches did, actually. How's your ankle?"

"Doing great. Gus had this guy Don work on it and it was like a miracle."

"Don's amazing. I used to have this bad knee. For years, it killed me. One of those football injuries they say will never go away. But Don worked on it once and it's been pain-free ever since. Simply amazing. So, are you ready? It's going to be a big week for you coming up."

"I know. Biggest week of my life. But I think I'm ready."

"Do you have faith that you will make the team?" Coach Ken asked as he cocked his head to the side and squinted.

"Yes, I do, Coach."

"What do you have faith in, Martin?" he said, lowering his voice.

"Myself," Martin responded.

"What else?"

Martin paused. "In you, Coach. I have faith in you. You've given me such a boost."

"And what else?" Coach asked, waiting for the right answer.

But Martin didn't give it, and Coach knew he couldn't force it. He just shook his head and told Martin he would see him later. He had become a fisher of men and he knew that you had to wait until they were ready. Try to catch them too soon and you would lose them. Martin just wasn't ready to bite yet, and no matter how much he wanted Martin to have faith, Martin was the one that had to desperately want it, seek it, and receive it. He knew Martin needed to have faith in more than himself and in an old line coach like him. While he could guide him in the right direction, Martin needed so much more than anything he could provide. It was time for a fishing trip, he decided.

Chapter 27

The Fishing Trip

That evening Martin received a text on his cell phone from Coach Ken. It said: "Meet me at the office at 5:00 A.M."

Martin sent a text back: "5:00 A.M., even the roosters don't get up that early."

Coach replied with a final text: "Those who are willing to pay the price do. See you at 5:00 A.M."

When Martin arrived at the office, still half-asleep, Coach told him they were going on a little trip. They walked to the parking lot and got in Coach Ken's truck.

Martin fell asleep as Coach Ken drove about a half hour to his favorite fishing spot at a nearby lake. When they arrived, Martin woke up, asking groggily, "Where are we?"

"Fishing. We are at one of my favorite spots on earth. Some call it a lake. I call it God's country. Now grab this fishing pole and follow me," he said as they walked through a long and winding trail until they reached a boat that was tied to a dock.

"Get in," Coach said as Martin climbed awkwardly into the boat. Coach Ken got the boat started and off they went to a quiet spot in the middle of the lake.

Martin just sat there holding the pole, wondering what in the world he was doing on a boat in the middle of a lake at 5:30 in the morning when he should be sleeping, getting ready for a full day of practice.

"You ever been fishing before?" Coach Ken asked, even though from the way Martin held a fishing pole it was clear he had no idea what he was doing.

"Only fishing I've ever done is in my bathtub," Martin quipped.

Coach Ken laughed. "Well, it's real simple. Just hold your pole up, keep your line in the water, and let the fish come to you," he said. "I made it easy and even put the bait on the hook for you. Now simply be still. It's very relaxing."

"More like boring," Martin thought.

"And a few rules for fishing you need to know."

Martin wasn't in the mood for any rules, especially at 5:30 in the morning, but he acted like he was interested.

"First, positive people catch more fish. Stay positive," Coach Ken said.

"Second, seize the moment. When the fish bite, that's when you have to be ready. With fishing, you spend most of your time baiting and waiting and only a brief moment actually catching the fish. When the moment happens, you must be ready. A lot like sports. And the third and final rule, don't leave fish to find fish."

"That's it?" Martin asked.

"That's it," Coach answered. "That's all I got."

"Sounds good to me," answered Martin, who wondered when they were going to head back to training camp. He was starting to wake up and this was the last place he wanted to be.

"So, Martin," Coach said, clearly changing the direction of the conversation. "I have an important question to ask you."

"What's that?" Martin asked.

"What are you afraid of?"

"What do you mean?" Martin asked.

"I mean exactly what I'm saying," Coach answered. "What do you fear?"

"Nothing," Martin said as he shifted uncomfortably in his seat and wondered why Coach Ken was asking him this.

"Come on, Martin. Everyone has fears. Everyone is scared of something. The best all have fear, but they over-come it. They conquer it. They succeed in spite of it. So, what are you afraid of?"

"I'm not sure," said Martin. "I haven't really thought about it."

"Well, you need to think about it," Coach countered. "To overcome your fear, you have to know what you are up against. To beat your enemy, you must know your enemy. Average people shy away from their fears. They either ignore them or hide from them. However, the best seek them out and face them with the intent of conquering them. So, I'm going to ask you again, Martin, what are you afraid of?"

Martin still wasn't sure what to say. He knew he was scared of his mother dying, but he didn't want to tell anyone. Other than that he couldn't think of what he was afraid of besides his ankle not being full strength.

"I'm scared of my ankle not healing," he said, hoping to give Coach Ken something so he would move to another subject.

But Coach Ken wasn't about to take the bait. "Oh, come on, Martin, you have to give me more than that. Life's too short to be lived superficially. If you want to be the best, it's time to go deeper, and it starts by uncovering and exposing your fears.

"So, I'm going to ask you again. What are you afraid of?"

Martin felt the knot once again in his chest and in his stomach. He didn't want to say it. He didn't want to tell anyone. Doing so would make it more real than he wanted it to be, but he had to give Coach something.

"My Momma," Martin said. "She's sick. Has a bad heart. Needs surgery that I don't have the money to pay for yet, and I'm afraid of her dying. There, I said it," he admitted. Martin shook his head as tears welled up in his eyes.

Coach acted like he didn't know, but he did know. It was their job as coaches to know as much about their players, their families, and their histories as possible. He felt horrible that such a young man had to carry such a heavy responsibility and burden, but he also knew that everyone carries a burden with them through life. Everyone is tested with challenges beyond their control. Everyone has experiences that will reveal their weakness and brokenness, and yet it was this brokenness that would ultimately make a person seek wholeness and the ultimate healing.

"I'm sorry about your mother," Coach said as he put his hand on Martin's shoulder.

"Yeah, me, too," Martin said.

"Is there anything I can do?" Coach asked.

"Get her a new heart," Martin wanted to say, but he knew that was his job. He couldn't put that on anyone else. So he just said, "No, I got it covered."

"And what bigger fear does this bring up for you?" Coach Ken asked, knowing that there was still yet a bigger fear that Martin needed to realize and confront. He knew that there were fears, and then there were really big fears. And it was smaller, more obvious fears that would lead you to the bigger hidden fears if you followed the trail.

Unfortunately, Martin wasn't ready to go there. He hit a wall, shut down, and said, "I don't know, Coach," and made it clear with this body language that he didn't want to talk anymore. After talking about his mother he felt exposed and vulnerable.

"That's okay," Coach said. "We've made some progress. But remember, if you want to be the best, you have to know what you are up against. Not just one fear. Not just your smallest fear. But your biggest fear. And then you must overcome all of them. That's the seventh trait of the best of the best.

7. The Best overcome their fear.

"So, I want you to really think about what your fears are," Coach continued. "When you know, come talk to me. But until then there's nothing more to teach and we can't continue through the playbook. We must first confront the issue of fear before moving on. It goes to the heart of greatness. It's the ultimate battle. Too many people retreat from this battle and fail to achieve their dreams. But those that succeed, those that reach the pinnacle of greatness, are able to face this battle and win. And you don't have to do it alone. I'm in the trenches with you, Martin. And God is with you. Just come to me when you are ready." Martin nodded, thinking that he hated fishing more than he thought he would. "And one more thing," Coach added, "I'll be praying for your mother. I have a feeling she's going to be alright."

"Thanks," said Martin, wishing he had never said anything about her.

As they headed back to the dock Coach knew it had been a good decision to take Martin fishing. Though they didn't have the breakthrough he had hoped for, he knew that Martin was uncomfortable, and this was a good thing. Sometimes a man has to be isolated and have no way out before he is willing to look within and above. Sometimes he has to go through darkness to want to see the light. He had to be desperate. Unfortunately, Martin wasn't desperate enough yet.

Chapter 28

Story and Belief

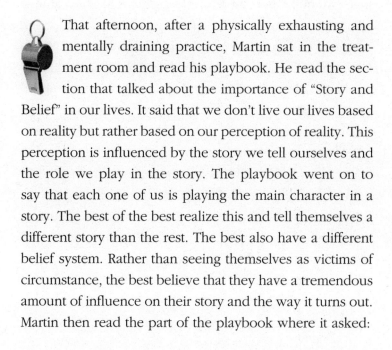

That afternoon, after a physically exhausting and mentally draining practice, Martin sat in the treatment room and read his playbook. He read the section that talked about the importance of "Story and Belief" in our lives. It said that we don't live our lives based on reality but rather based on our perception of reality. This perception is influenced by the story we tell ourselves and the role we play in the story. The playbook went on to say that each one of us is playing the main character in a story. The best of the best realize this and tell themselves a different story than the rest. The best also have a different belief system. Rather than seeing themselves as victims of circumstance, the best believe that they have a tremendous amount of influence on their story and the way it turns out. Martin then read the part of the playbook where it asked:

> *If your life was a movie, what kind of movie it would be? How would you describe it? Drama? Comedy? Love story? Or inspirational tale?*

In this movie, what role are you playing? Victim? Bystander? Fighter? Underdog? Hero?

In reading this, Martin realized that though he had always thought of his life as an inspirational tale, lately it had become a drama, and instead of the hero, he was playing the victim. His mother, on the other hand, was living both an inspirational tale and a love story. She had so much love and hope that she refused to see her life through the eyes of a victim. In her eyes she was a lover, a fighter, and an overcomer. She believed in a happy ending. Martin knew that he needed to be more like her, and he vowed to change his story. He vowed to see his life as an inspirational tale. No longer was he a victim; from now on, he would be a hero.

But as everyone knows, every hero in every story must come face to face with his nemesis and overcome certain tests to define himself and create his success. And unfortunately for Martin, over the next few days he would face some of the biggest tests, and the greatest nemesis of his life.

Chapter 29

Tests

In his decision to be a hero, Martin forgot the part of the story where the hero relies on the help of others to defeat the enemy. Instead Martin decided to go it alone. During the next few days he played some of the worst football of his life. He was scared of getting injured again, and this affected his focus and performance. He didn't think quickly or run quickly—and both had been essential to his success. Without them he was like any average football player. He missed several passes thrown his way, messed up his blocking assignments, and even fumbled a few kickoffs. He spent more time worrying about getting injured than he did trying to impress the coaches. Not only did he fail, but he failed to impress.

To make matters worse, Shawna called and told him that Momma was feeling more tired than usual and the doctor said this was not a good sign. Though Momma was her usual confident self, Martin couldn't help but worry. The only good news was that he spoke with several sports agents and they all agreed to give him a signing advance upon making the team, and this advance would easily cover Momma's surgery. Once he signed the contract with the team, he would be able to pay the agents back. Two important things had to happen, however, for Martin to receive his advance: one, he had to choose a sports agent, and two—and more important—he had to make the team, which was looking more and more unlikely due to the way he was playing.

Instead of looking like someone who was trying to make the team, Martin looked like he belonged back in the training room. Instead of playing to win, he was playing to lose. Instead of going for his dream, Martin was playing it safe, trying not to get injured. Instead of going for broke, Martin was trying not to make mistakes. It wasn't a recipe for success. It was a recipe for disaster.

Chapter 30

Pressure

It was the day before their final preseason game. It would be the end of training camp, and everyone knew this meant that the final cut was almost here. The pressure was at an all-time high, and Martin was in the training room icing his ankle. He looked down at his bracelet and the words "Heal Strong" and hoped that his ankle would hold up for him. He was devastated at how he had played the last few days in practice, but he knew that if he had a great game tomorrow night, everything would be fine.

Gus came over and asked him how everything was going. Martin said fine and thanked Gus for all he did in helping get him his ankle ready.

"No problem," Gus said. "But as I told you, Martin, the mind is more important than your ankle. How you really doing?" he asked, clearly concerned.

"I'm fine," Martin reiterated.

"Coach Ken been giving you good advice?" Gus asked.

"Great advice," Martin said. "Really great advice. We just got stuck on the fear thing, that's all."

"Well, that's a pretty big thing to get stuck on," Gus said. "You know, having been around all these years, there's one thing I noticed. There's so much pressure and competition at this level that you have to turn to something. Some guys, unfortunately, turn to drugs, alcohol, and girls. Other guys turn into themselves and implode because the pressure is too great. Some turn to people that they can count on, while some turn to people they can't. Others turn to their faith. The point is, no matter what, everyone turns to something. Just make sure you turn to the right things. Okay?"

"Okay," answered Martin, who was thankful for Gus's advice. He knew the one thing that he could turn to lately was Coach Ken and his playbook. He hadn't read it in a few days and decided to get back to it. So that night, the night before the biggest game of his life, he read the playbook, and it was exactly what he needed to understand what was holding him back and what he needed to do to be his best on game day.

Chapter 31

Seize the Moment

Martin read ahead in the playbook to the eighth trait of the best of the best and it said:

 8. The Best seize the moment.

The best seize the moment because they don't allow their fear of failure to define them. They know this fear exists, and they overcome it. Their faith is greater than any score, performance, or outcome. Even if they lose, they are still on the path to greatness. And even if they fail, they are one step closer to the perfection they seek.

Ironically, even though the best have a dream and a vision within their sights, it is the journey, not the destination, that matters most to them. The moment is more important than any success or failure. The moment is the success. The moment is the reward.

When the best are in the midst of their performance, they are not thinking "What if I win?" or "What if I lose?" They are not thinking "What if I make a mistake or miss the shot?" They are not interested in what the moment produces but are only concerned with what they produce in the moment. When all eyes are watching, they know that this is the moment they have been preparing and waiting for. Rather than hiding from pressure, they rise to the occasion. As a result, the best define the moment rather than letting the moment define them. To seize the moment, don't let your failure define you; let it fuel you. Don't run from fear; face it and embrace it. Don't let fear rob you of your love and joy for the game; let it push you into the moment and beyond yourself. Let it inspire you to live and work each day as though it were your last.

Don't let the moment define you. You define the moment. Define it by knowing that your practice and preparation have prepared you well. Define it with your mental strength, faith, and confidence. Define it by knowing that regardless of the outcome, you have given your very best.

Everyone talks about destiny. Everyone searches for it, not realizing that each and every moment is your destiny. Make every moment of your life count. Realize that this is your one shot, yet don't focus on the result or the outcome of the shot. Jut focus on the shot.

Don't focus on the past, and don't look to the future. Focus on the now. Success, rewards, accolades, *fame, and fortune are merely byproducts for those who are able to seize the moment—not those who look beyond it. Ironically, to enjoy success you must not focus on it. Rather, you must focus on the process that produces success.*

You are more than your successes. You are more than your failures. You are who you are in the moment. Enjoy it. Live it. Make the most of it. Make it yours.

After reading this it became very clear to Martin why Coach Ken was so adamant about discussing fear. And now it was even clearer how this fear was impacting his performance over the past few days. When he arrived at training camp there was no pressure and no fear. No one expected him to make the team. But with his great performance there came expectations from the coaches and himself. Now, rather than creating success on the field, he was more worried about what failure meant off the field. Rather than just playing football and enjoying the moment, he was worried about his mother, his ankle, and all the negative consequences of not making the team. "It's ironic," he thought, "that I became a success by playing with nothing to lose. But now that I feel like there is something to lose, I'm no longer a success."

He remembered how this happened in college one year. His team, which was virtually ignored by all the television commentators and sports shows, came from the bottom of the ranks to become a top-twenty football team. But as soon as the spotlight was on them, the players started to focus on the hype they received. They started to believe their own press clippings. They lost their focus. They lost their way. They focused on the outcome, not the process. Instead of playing like a team that had nothing to lose, they played like a team that was worried about losing. As soon as this happened their performance suffered and, as is often the case, the spotlight then moved on to another team.

He knew that the best perform their best in the face of pressure, not in the absence of it. Anyone could perform great when there were no expectations, no pressure, no consequences, and no spotlight, but Martin knew that if he truly wanted to be the best, that meant performing at his highest level when the spotlight was on him and everything was on the line.

He had allowed his fear of failure to define him, and he knew what he needed to do. He needed to stop thinking about the consequences of his performance and just focus on the performance. He needed to focus on the *now* and seize the moment.

From now on he decided it was all about making the most of the moment. This was a good thing, because tomorrow night was the team's final preseason game, and it would be the biggest moment of his life.

Chapter 32

The Breaking Point

It was game day, and though many of the players slept in, Martin woke up early. Over the past few weeks he had gotten use to waking up early, and now, despite his desire to sleep in, he was wide awake. He walked to the treatment room, said hello to Gus, and headed over to Coach Ken's office. He was excited to tell him about the realization he had last night. When he knocked, no one answered. So he walked in to see Coach Ken sitting at his desk, mouthing words with his eyes closed.

"What are you doing?" Martin asked.

"Meditating," he answered.

"Meditating on what?"

"On *The Word*. Been doing it every day since *The Day*," Coach said.

"What's *The Day?*" Martin asked. "You gotta tell me."

"I'll tell you soon, Martin. Just not time yet. But you'll know soon enough."

"So, what's with the meditating?" Martin asked.

115

"Well, ever since *The Day* I realized how important it is to start your day off right. Instead of letting the world create you, you create your world. Instead of starting your morning by turning on the news, I say consider taking a walk of prayer. Instead of looking down at the paper, look up to the heavens. And instead of listening to all those sports commentators say how great or bad you are, simply walk outside, close your eyes, smell the fresh air, take a few deep breaths, and discover the real peace you seek. I always tell my girls that each day they must stay positive, do their best to succeed and have faith in a brighter and better future. I believe this is the antidote to fear, and what we truly need to succeed in this world."

Martin was glad that coach brought up the issue of fear, because it was exactly what he came to talk to him about. "Yeah, about that," Martin said. "About the fear you said I needed to know and overcome. I read the part in the playbook about seizing the moment, and it hit me what my fear is. You want to know what it is."

"Of course I do," said Coach. He was both surprised and thrilled that Martin wanted to talk about it. He had almost given up on it as a lost cause, but just when you give up hope, God and people will always surprise you, he thought to himself. "What do you have for me?"

"Well, Coach," Martin said. "I realized that I fear failure. I'm scared of not making the team. I'm fearful of what this will mean in terms of my future and my mother's future."

"This is big, Martin," Coach said with an enthusiastic smile Martin hadn't seen before. "This is really big." He had been waiting for this moment ever since their first conversation. "We're excavating now," he added. "Each fear reveals a deeper fear. Your fear about your mom's health brought up your fear of *failure,* and this fear leads to your fear of *not being enough,* which reveals your ultimate fear of *not being loved.* So many people have this fear, Martin. Especially great performers. They get so tied into their accomplishments and success they wonder if anyone will love them for who they are rather than what they do. But what they and you need to know is that you are loved by God, and this is the ultimate answer to your ultimate fear. Do you know how I know this?"

"How?" asked Martin, who was still uncomfortable talking about his fears. The conversation had already gone on longer than he had hoped.

"Because love casts out all fear. If you're a mom, you wouldn't walk across a busy highway for fear of getting hit by a car. But if your child ran into the street you would run after her. Because love casts out all fear. Love is more powerful than fear."

"But how come I don't feel God's love? Why isn't it casting out my fear?" Martin asked.

"Because you haven't opened the door to your heart. God's knocking, but you're not letting Him in. The fact is, if you knew who walked alongside you, with all the love in the universe, and you knew who carried you through all the challenging times in your life to where you are right now, you wouldn't know fear. You wouldn't be afraid. You would accept and receive this love, and it would cast out your fears—big and small."

"But I am afraid," Martin admitted.

"That's because pride keeps you separate from the love of God. Pride causes the ripple of fear in your life, and all your fears big and small can be traced back to it. Instead of trying to be one with God, pride says 'I can be my own God. I can do it alone.' This often makes you work really hard as you seek to gain love through your accomplishments and success, but ultimately causes you to crash and burn when you realize that all the material success and accolades in the world are not enough to fill the void. They are not enough to eliminate the anxiety you feel. They're not enough to keep you from seeking something more. That's because you were not created to be separate from the love of God. You were made to be one with it. But know this: God doesn't keep us separate from this love. Pride does.

"And so you keep working, keep striving, and keep pushing. You keep working toward getting the love you seek, and the harder you work, the more elusive it becomes. It's ironic how pride often pushes you to be the best, but also keeps you from it. That's because it pushes you toward God's love and away from it at the same time. You know you were created for more, but you don't know how to get it. You're broken, so you seek wholeness, but your pride keeps you from the ultimate healing. Then you hit your breaking point. Then you realize that you can't do it alone. Then you join the ranks of all the people, including the best of the best, who have come to a point in their lives when they realize they can't do it by themselves.

"Honestly, I think that's why we strive, Martin. It's the ultimate quest. We strive because God knows that in the striving we will push ourselves to the point where we come to the reality that we need something more—that our will isn't big enough—that our strength isn't strong enough. It is then that we seek God with our whole heart. It is at this breaking point when we realize that we must tap into a power greater than ourselves. *This allows us to become more than what we want to be. It inspires us and moves us to become everything God intends for us to be.* The quest for greatness then becomes a joy rather than a burden. And this is the ninth trait of the best of the best."

 ## 9. The Best tap into a power greater than themselves.

"No one ever talked to me before about this," Martin said, trying to wrap his mind around everything Coach was saying.

"That's because it's not politically correct to talk about it. We celebrate all the famous people who created positive change in the world because of their faith, and then we're not supposed to talk about the faith that greatness requires. The fact is, you can't talk about greatness without talking about God. It would be like talking about breathing without mentioning the importance of air. We were created to do great things. It's all part of the plan. In fact, if you asked the people who changed the world throughout history, they would all tell you that they tapped into the greatest and ultimate power. They would tell you that it was their faith that carried them through the adversities, the pain, and the suffering. They would tell you that they got a sense of the divine on their march to greatness. They would tell you that they became a conductor instead of a resistor."

"What's a conductor and a resistor?" asked Martin.

"According to one of my favorite writers, John Ortberg, it has to do with the world of atoms and electrons. He says that resistors *hold on* and conductors *let go*. A resistor doesn't want to let go of its electrons. It's stingy. It holds on to them, and in doing so the resistor has little or no electrical current moving through it, and thus has limited power. The conductor, by contrast, is willing to let go of its electrons. In doing so it doesn't generate its own power; it is simply a conduit. However, it generates an enormous amount of power from the current that flows through it. The greater the current, the greater the power that will be radiated by the conductor.

"In spiritual terms we can say that resistors rely on their own power so their power is limited. Their pride keeps them separate from the ultimate power source. Conductors, by contrast, empty themselves of their pride and allow the ultimate power to flow through them. They become a conduit and a vessel for the greatest power source in the world. And so the measure of someone's power can be determined by how much they are willing to let go and how great a vessel they allow themselves to become."

"So how do I do this?" Martin asked. "How do I become a conductor?"

"You let go. You surrender. You give all your pain and fear and anxiety, and all your junk to God, and you say 'I can't do it alone. I need you.' You stop being a resistor and stop trying to do it all yourself. You allow the power behind all of creation to move through you."

"But it's so hard to let go," Martin said as tears welled up in his eyes.

"I know," said Coach Ken. "It's the hardest thing in the world to do. We are so used to being in control that we're afraid of what might happen if we take our hands off of the steering wheel and let God drive our life. We think we'll fall apart, but it's really the beginning of our life coming together. Jeff Gordon, the racecar driver, once told me that every time he tried to direct his own life, it fell apart. But when he let God drive the way, it all worked out. And if a racecar driver can say that, then so can you. So, are you ready to surrender it all? It's time to give up being a resistor. Say it with me. 'I can't do it alone. I need you, God.'"

Martin tried, but he couldn't do it. He was too uncomfortable and embarrassed to let go and too comfortable with his junk.

Coach Ken repeated, "'I can't do it alone. I need you.' Say it, Martin."

Martin grimaced and squirmed as he sat in a chair and put his face in his hands. "No," Martin yelled. "I can't do it."

Coach Ken grabbed Martin's hand and clutched it in his two giant hands. He knew this was pride making its last stand. He repeated, this time in a whisper. "Say it, Martin. 'I can't do it alone. I need you.'"

This time Martin said it, barely, under his breath, as he clenched Coach Ken's hand and fell to the floor on his knees. "Say it, Martin, 'I am not in control, God. You are in control. And I trust in your plan for my life.'"

Martin resisted all he could, but then all at once the tears started flowing and he sobbed and sobbed and sobbed as he let go of Coach's hand and punched the air a few times. He fell to the floor, and with him he brought all his memories and all his pain and all his fear. When everything was falling apart around him, he was the one who had to keep it together. When his father died, everyone turned to him. When his mother got sick, everyone turned to him. When something went wrong in the family, they turned to him. Everyone turned to him, and now after years of relying on himself and his mother, Martin finally turned to God.

He banged the floor and clenched his fist and said, "Okay, I give it all to you. I surrender." Again, he clenched his fist and repeated, "I surrender." Raising his voice, he repeated, "I can't do it alone. I need you. Please save me." And then something happened. He stopped banging the floor. Then, he closed his eyes, thought of his wonderful mother and said a silent prayer—the one he said each night as a young boy—when he saw God as a relationship rather than a religion. And in that moment he felt this amazing feeling. Goosebumps covered his body and he felt a kind of grace and peace like he had never known. He felt like the weight of the world had been lifted from his body. Like Atlas had taken the world off his shoulders. He rose from the floor, and Coach Ken gave him a hug. A man hug. The kind of hug that men of faith weren't afraid to give each other. And then Coach Ken grabbed Martin's hands in his and looked in his eyes and said, "Don't forget this moment. You're not a resistor anymore. You're a conductor now."

"I won't," Martin said. How could he forget? How could he forget the small voice inside him that spoke loud and clear, *Let go. I am with you. Have faith in Me.* How could he forget the greatest feeling he had ever known?

It was a voice and a feeling that Coach Ken had seen change countless lives. It was a voice and a feeling that lead people from desperation to surrender to greatness. It had been a while since he had seen someone resist with such pride. Most of the people he had worked with didn't have such a dramatic transformation. But he also knew that some of the biggest resistors became some of the biggest conductors, if they allowed themselves to become vessels. He hoped this would be the case with Martin.

Chapter 33

The Spotlight

 Everybody who strives to be the best gets the opportunity to live in that moment where the spotlight is on them, and the world is watching, and they have the opportunity to win or lose the game for their team. Some run and hide from this light. It's too bright for them. But the best shine under it. The best are the ones who make the plays so their team can win.

Martin stood in the end zone waiting for the kickoff. He knew the spotlight was on him, and he was ready. His ankle was taped. He wore his lucky #11 jersey and he had eyeblack under his eyes with the words *Phil* under the right eye and *4:13* under his left eye. His mind was focused and his spirit was strong. He was bolstered by the fact that his momma was at the game. She'd told him she wouldn't miss it for the world. And the love of his life, Shawna, was with her. They planned to get married after training camp, regardless of whether or not Martin made the team.

He spent the day recharging his batteries from his emotional morning with Coach Ken. But surprisingly, it didn't take long, and at this moment he felt more energized than he had in a long, long time. This was a good thing because as he received the kickoff and dropped the ball, he would need that energy to avoid getting pulverized. With the ball on the ground and the other team racing toward him, he slipped and thought to himself, I blew it. I blew it. But then he heard a whisper that said, *Get up. Get up.* He raced to his feet, picked up the ball, and ran up field as fast as he could. One tackler raced by him. Another bounced off him. He made a fake to the left, then ran to the right and saw a wide gap open up. With lightning speed he ran through the gap, made one more fake, and all that was left between him and the end zone was the kicker. Martin raced past the kicker, but just as he was in the clear the kicker leaped, threw up his arm, and hit Martin's left leg just enough to trip him up. Martin fell to the ground, but not before he made it to the other team's 40-yard line. He didn't score a touchdown, but once again Martin had electrified the crowd.

Throughout the game he would get many more opportunities to shine, and he made the most of them. The coaches commented to each other via the headsets that he was like a different player from the one they saw practicing this week. He ran the ball hard, protected his quarterback on pass plays, and caught a few passes out of the backfield. When it was all said and done, Martin had a great game. But so did the other rookie vying for a spot on the team. In the eyes of most observers, they played equally well. The only difference was that the other rookie scored two short yardage touchdowns and Martin returned and excelled on kickoffs. It seemed that with every kickoff return, he was one tackle away from running it back for a touchdown. And every time Martin touched the ball the crowd held its collective breath, expecting something exciting to happen. He was quickly becoming a fan favorite. He only hoped that he was the coaching staff's favorite, as they made their final cuts tomorrow.

Chapter 34

Celebration

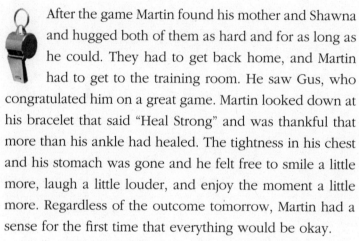 After the game Martin found his mother and Shawna and hugged both of them as hard and for as long as he could. They had to get back home, and Martin had to get to the training room. He saw Gus, who congratulated him on a great game. Martin looked down at his bracelet that said "Heal Strong" and was thankful that more than his ankle had healed. The tightness in his chest and his stomach was gone and he felt free to smile a little more, laugh a little louder, and enjoy the moment a little more. Regardless of the outcome tomorrow, Martin had a sense for the first time that everything would be okay.

Later that night Martin accepted an invitation from some of the veterans to join them for a late dinner at a jazz club. Martin, of course, couldn't say no. Plus it was the last night of training camp, and it was reason enough to celebrate. He had heard that it was a sign that you would likely make the team when the veterans asked you to go out with them, although he had also heard stories from players that were invited out by veterans only to get cut the following day.

And while the players celebrated and Martin enjoyed a steady diet of steak, sparkling water, and jazz, he decided it was time to leave the party. He was tired after a long day and wanted to head back and get some sleep. He walked down the street in search of a taxi, and eventually came to the stoop of a church, where he plopped down on the steps outside, closed his eyes, and said a prayer. He prayed for his mother. He thanked God for Coach Ken. And he prayed for good news tomorrow.

In the middle of his prayer a voice came from behind him and startled him. "Whatcha doing on my steps?" a homeless man said as he approached.

"Praying," Martin said. "It's a church after all, right?"

"You got that right," the homeless man said. "You don't know God's all you need until God's all you got."

"You got that right," Martin said, as he gave the man five dollars, walked down the steps to the street, and caught a taxicab back to the team complex.

Chapter 35

Final Cuts

 The call came early in the morning—too early for Martin, who was in the middle of a deep sleep and an enjoyable dream. He didn't want to get up. Today he wanted to sleep till noon. The team wasn't practicing today and his tired body was finally letting him sleep in. But the voice on the other end of the line told him to be in Coach's office in 30 minutes. So he got dressed and made his way to the team facility where he would soon learn his fate.

As he waited outside the head coach's office, one of the other players walked out as the head coach patted him on the back and told him that he wished him luck and would be happy to make a few calls for him. Clearly, the player had not received good news. Martin only hoped his news would be better. He walked in, sat down, and prepared himself, knowing that whatever decision coach would share, he knew he had given his best. No matter what news he heard, he wasn't going to give up. He was committed to being the best here or with another team that could benefit from his talent.

But Martin wasn't going to another team. The head coach told him that it was a difficult choice but after last night's game the coaching staff decided to keep both Martin and the other rookie running back. They both made the final cut. They both made the team.

He could hardly contain himself as all the pressure and all the excitement exploded into one big giant *yes!* that he yelled at the top of his lungs. "That's one of the things we love about you, Martin. Your passion. Don't ever lose it. Keep the fire burning and you'll be in this league a long time," Coach said as he shook Martin's hand and congratulated him on making the team.

Martin walked out of the office a foot taller than when he had walked in. He couldn't believe it. He was living his dream. He was officially a professional football player. He called his mother and it was impossible to have a conversation with her—not because she wasn't feeling well but because she was cheering at the top of her lungs with excitement.

"Take it easy, Momma," he said. "Take it easy. I don't want anything to happen to you before your operation. So you call that doctor and you tell them you're ready for the operation. Schedule it soon. Money's not a problem anymore."

Coach Ken was next on his list, and he ran to his office to talk about the news. Of course, Coach Ken already knew, but talking to him about it made it more real for some reason. When he arrived Coach Ken was eating another fish taco.

"I know," Martin said. "Ever since *The Day*.

"I made it," Martin cheered. "I made it. This is one of the best days of my life. I can't thank you enough, Coach."

"Don't thank me," Coach Ken said as he clapped his hands slowly, showing his support. "You did it. You are the one who seized the moment. You practiced, you prepared. You gave your best, and that's all that anyone could ask for. I'm thrilled for you and I'm proud of you. But now you have to ask yourself, *Now what?*"

"Now we become the best of the best," Martin said, as if there was no other option.

"And *then what?*" coach asked as he cocked his head and squinted his eyes.

"Then I become a Pro Bowler like you. Isn't this what you taught me? To strive to become the best of the best."

"And *then what?*" coach asked again.

Martin didn't know what to say.

"You see where I'm going with this, Martin. In our pursuit of greatness, it's easy to become self-consumed and self-focused. Because you have to give all of who you are to become everything you're meant to be. Yet if you look back you'll realize that you didn't do it alone. There were people and coaches and teachers that guided you along the way. They left a legacy, and that legacy is you. And so when you think about *now what,* I want you to think about what it means in terms of not just your greatness, but also the greatness you leave in others."

Chapter 36

Leave a Legacy

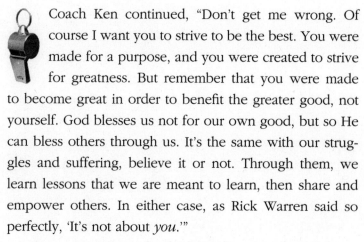 Coach Ken continued, "Don't get me wrong. Of course I want you to strive to be the best. You were made for a purpose, and you were created to strive for greatness. But remember that you were made to become great in order to benefit the greater good, not yourself. God blesses us not for our own good, but so He can bless others through us. It's the same with our struggles and suffering, believe it or not. Through them, we learn lessons that we are meant to learn, then share and empower others. In either case, as Rick Warren said so perfectly, 'It's not about *you*.'"

"In your striving to be the best, then, you must ask not what your greatness means to you, but what impact does it make on others? The success you create now is temporary, but the legacy you leave is eternal. Thinking about this legacy fuels you with a bigger purpose."

"That's why you told me making the team was good, but being the best is a life mission," Martin said. It was all becoming clear.

"Exactly," Coach responded. "You know, every year I tell my guys. Don't focus on the contract and the money. The best are driven by something bigger. It can't be about the contract. That's not what drives the best to be the best. The best are driven by a bigger purpose, and this purpose fuels them. Now, I can't tell someone what their purpose is, but I can tell them that the best are most energized when they are using their gifts and talents for a purpose beyond themselves. You can see it in their eyes and in their passion and enthusiasm for the game and the way they play on the field and carry themselves off it. Money doesn't create that kind of energy, but purpose does. Sure, money might make you perform well in the short term, but it won't inspire you to be the best and strive for greatness over the long term. The best are driven by much, much more. Average players are motivated by the paycheck. The great ones are inspired to leave a legacy. And this doesn't apply to just football. It applies to every job in the world.

"That's why the tenth trait of the best of the best is that they leave a legacy."

 ## 10. The Best leave a legacy.

Martin looked at the playbook as Coach spoke more passionately about this than anything he had ever taught him.

He concluded, "You leave a legacy by living and working with a bigger purpose. You leave a legacy by making your life about more than just you. You leave a legacy by moving from success to significance. For me, I came to a point where I realized that my success was for a bigger reason. I was given this platform not for me but to better others. Ever since *The Day*. I knew I was meant for more."

"What's *The Day?*" Martin asked, hoping Coach Ken would finally tell him. "I'm not leaving here until you tell me."

"Well, I'm happy to tell you. Not because you won't leave, but because it's time." It was definitely time, and Martin was about to learn why Coach Ken had spent so much time teaching the playbook to him.

Chapter 37

The Day

"The Day is the day that I died, Martin. It was my first year of coaching. There I was in my office eating a loaded Italian sub, and then *bam*. I'm hovering over my body watching myself lie there on the floor."

"Are you serious?" Martin asked in amazement. "You really died and saw yourself on the floor? For real?"

"Yes, Martin," said Coach Ken. "I really died."

"Did you see the light?" Martin asked. "You always hear about people seeing the light when they die and come back to life."

"No, I didn't see any light. But I heard a voice. A loud, clear, booming voice that said, *Why are you persecuting my men? Stop condemning them. Stop bringing them down. Lift them up. Speak truth into them. Bring out the best in them.*

"Next thing I know I'm in a hospital room and the doctors tell me that I had been dead for 20 minutes. No brain damage. No heart problem. Nothing, except a craving for fish tacos. Hard to believe, huh?"

"Yeah," Martin said.

"They called it a miracle. From then on, I was like a new person. I felt different. I had always felt like I was in the first quarter of my life and I had three-quarters to go. After *The Day* I felt that I needed to live my life as if it were the fourth quarter, because I wasn't sure when the game was going to end. I knew it was time to change my ways and the ways I coached. I was a 300-pound jerk who never said one positive word to the players. I expected them to play the game the way I did, and so I coached the way I was coached. But after *The Day*, I knew I couldn't run people over any more. Instead I needed to invite them on my bus. I needed to bring out the best in them by sharing the best within me.

"I started eating healthy, lots of fish, started running, took a walk of prayer every morning, and one day during my walk I had the idea for the playbook. Right then I put it together and started to share it. So, when you first asked me why I wanted to help you, now you know this is why. It was because the day I died, I was given a new life, and I wanted to do more and give more with the life I had been given."

Martin was stunned. Coach Ken's words affected him in a positive way. He realized that everyone needed a positive and supportive team to be his best. No one does it alone. He thought of all the people that God had put on his path to help him over the years and realized that he was indeed a product of their support, love, and guidance. And during training camp, the biggest test and challenge of his life, God gave him the greatest and most important teacher he

140

had ever had—and the one he needed most. Coach Ken had become more than a coach. In a short time, he had become a friend and even more like a father. He stepped closer to Coach Ken and thanked him for all he had done for him and taught him. He gave him a hug and said, "I'll see you tomorrow."

Chapter 38

The Coin

 When Martin arrived to the team complex the next day, the mood was somber. Martin couldn't figure out why. It was the end of training camp and the beginning of a new season. The guys should be excited, he thought. He wondered if one of the players got in trouble last night, or perhaps someone was injured. He walked into the training room and Gus gave him an envelope and said it was from Coach Ken.

Martin opened it and inside was a coin that said *Be Your Best* on one side with *Seize the Moment* in the middle. On the other side it said *Greatness Is a Life Mission* around the border. In the middle it said *Leave a Legacy*.

"He wanted you to have this, Martin," Gus said.

"Why didn't he give it to me?" he asked as he saw tears come down Gus's face.

"He must have known," Gus answered. "He must have known. He just knew things. The guy just knew things."

At that moment all the players were called into the team meeting room, where the head coach addressed the team. "I have some bad news, guys, and I don't know how to say this. With sadness I must tell you that Coach Ken died last night." A collective cry filled the room. Some guys were too shocked to say anything; others, including Martin, burst into tears. For many of the guys on the team, Coach Ken had been more than a coach. He had been a friend, a counselor, and a father figure.

The head coach looked at his team and then as his hands trembled and he choked back tears he told them how Coach Ken had died peacefully in his sleep. The coach added, "Now, this is going to be tough, but we'll get through it like we get through everything. As a team. Coach Ken wouldn't want it any other way. We're dedicating the season to him. As you know, he wasn't just a fellow coach, he was a friend, and like a brother to me, and I know he was very special to all of you. We will miss him dearly, but remember what he would want most. He would want you to be your best, no matter what the circumstance. His funeral is in two days. Of course, take today off, and anyone who needs to talk, we're here, and the Chaplain is available."

As the players walked out of the team room, Martin didn't move. He was paralyzed by sadness. "How could this be?" he thought. "I just said goodbye to him yesterday. Peacefully in his sleep," he said to himself as he shook his head. The guy never slept. But just like that he was gone, and Martin lost another father figure in his life. He held the coin that Coach Ken had given him and looked at it as tears streamed down his face. He had cried more in the last week than he had in his entire life. He remembered all the wisdom Coach shared with him, and he knew right then what he needed to do.

Chapter 39

The Final Lesson

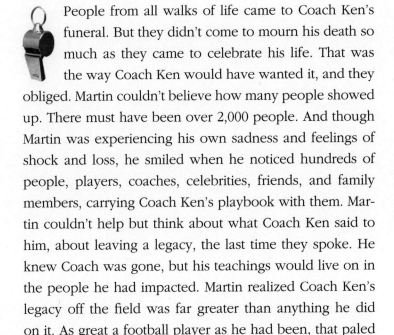 People from all walks of life came to Coach Ken's funeral. But they didn't come to mourn his death so much as they came to celebrate his life. That was the way Coach Ken would have wanted it, and they obliged. Martin couldn't believe how many people showed up. There must have been over 2,000 people. And though Martin was experiencing his own sadness and feelings of shock and loss, he smiled when he noticed hundreds of people, players, coaches, celebrities, friends, and family members, carrying Coach Ken's playbook with them. Martin couldn't help but think about what Coach Ken said to him, about leaving a legacy, the last time they spoke. He knew Coach was gone, but his teachings would live on in the people he had impacted. Martin realized Coach Ken's legacy off the field was far greater than anything he did on it. As great a football player as he had been, that paled in comparison to the greatness he achieved in the game of life.

During the funeral, Martin opened and looked at his playbook. However, he didn't need to read it to know the final lesson. And he didn't need Coach Ken to teach it to him in his own words. It was a lesson that Coach Ken had already taught him by the way he lived his life. Martin knew that the best make everyone around them better.

 11. The Best make everyone around them better.

They do this through their own pursuit of excellence and in the excellence they inspire in others. One person in pursuit of excellence raises the standards of everyone around them. And they do this both in their work and life.

Martin realized that for all the lessons he learned from Coach Ken, the most powerful lesson was Coach himself. Martin looked at Coach Ken's casket as reality began to sink in.

No one is going to live forever, and the outcome for all of us eventually leads to a funeral. "So what's the point?" he asked himself. And a small voice spoke to his heart and told him that the point is to strive to be your best and inspire others to be their best, because it's in the striving where you find greatness, not in the outcome. After all, even if you become the best in the world at what you do, it's short lived. Eventually someone will come along who is better. Being the best doesn't last. But the person you become and the impact you have on others are timeless.

Martin reasoned that in the debate of whether or not God cared about who won and lost football games, or whether God cared about sports at all, he determined that God didn't care who won or lost, but rather was interested in the stories and the lessons that we would learn from them. After all, why wouldn't God use one of the biggest stages in the world to teach us the most important life lessons? It was the ultimate reality show. But unlike reality show audiences and producers, God was less interested in outcomes and more interested in the character we develop along the way.

Martin decided that if he didn't become the best running back to ever play the game, that would be okay. What mattered most was that he strived to be the best he could be every day of his life, regardless of the outcome—and that he inspired excellence in others. It was a different standard of greatness than what the world thought, and that was fine with him.

He smiled and looked up and knew Coach Ken was looking down on him. "You knew I would eventually get it, didn't you?" he said, looking up to the heavens.

Yes, Coach Ken knew things. He knew that greatness was a life mission and that being the best really wasn't about being better than anyone else but about striving to be the best you could be and bringing out the best in others. Martin closed his eyes and said a prayer, and in that prayer the small voice spoke to him again and said, *It is time for a fishing trip.* He didn't know what it meant at the time, but months later, as he reflected on his time with Coach Ken, it would become very clear.

Chapter 40

A New Beginning

Martin stood on the sand about 25 yards form the ocean. It was January 1, his team had just made the playoffs, and Martin was being talked about as a possibility for rookie of the year. The players were given a few days off, and with his mother back to work and healthy again after a successful surgery, Martin and Shawna headed to the beach for a chance to relax and recharge. The wind was strong, the water was cold, and the sun was surprisingly bright. As Martin watched the waves crashing on shore, he saw a tall, fit man run by and could have sworn it was Coach Ken. It seemed like he saw him everywhere—in the airport, at the store, in the stands. It was hard to believe it had been only five months since his passing. To Martin it felt like it had been a lifetime already.

He stared at the ocean as he prepared to jump into the cold water—to take a symbolic plunge that this would be the year of *no fear*. By jumping into the ocean Martin was declaring that this year his faith would be bigger than his fear. It was to be his yearly ritual to remind himself to follow his passion, seize the moment, surrender, and stay one step ahead of the pride and fear that hovered around him. He had learned from Coach Ken that the antidote to fear is trust, and it is only a thought away. He knew that no one was going to push you over the chasm of struggle to the life that you want. God will nudge you and others will support you, but you must take the leap yourself. You must make this jump in your mind, with your heart, and then with your actions. You must make this jump with trust, determination, and faith. After all, they don't call it a leap of fear. They call it a *leap of faith* for a reason. And with faith he knew that you become a conduit for miracles. His momma had always told him so, but now he believed it.

He raced toward the water as his heart started pounding faster and faster. He feared the coldness more than he did any defense in the NFL. But he kept running, knowing that this was a moment he needed to seize. And as a wave came crashing toward him, he leaped over it and plunged into ocean.

He emerged invigorated and ready to take on all that life had to offer. The good, the bad, the joy, the pain, the defeats, and the triumphs, and most of all, the miracle of everyday life. He dried himself off and went to his car, opened the trunk, and threw the towel in a plastic bag next to the boxes of training camp coins and stacks of playbooks he recently had printed. He had added a message about Coach Ken and then he had hundreds of copies printed.

As soon as the season was over, he and Shawna were taking a trip around the country to colleges, high schools, and various audiences to share Coach Ken's lessons with as many people as possible. They called it their *fishing trip,* and it would be the first of many.

Martin knew that the lessons of training camp weren't just meant for football players and athletes, but for anyone who wanted to strive to be their best. After all, greatness is a life mission.

In the back of the playbook, Martin added the following dedication to Coach Ken:

Coach Ken was a father, a husband, a legendary football player, a coach, a teacher, a mentor, a friend, a brother, and a father figure to many. He pursued excellence throughout his life and empowered others to do the same. This playbook is the result of his quest to be a lifelong learner and leader, and his desire to inspire others to strive to be the best they can be. Coach Ken always said that greatness was a life mission, and we are thankful that through this playbook we are able to live and share his principles, teachings, and lessons. He was a blessing to the world and he will be dearly missed. In honor of Coach Ken we hope you will use this playbook to strive to be the best you can be and bring out the best in others.

The End

A New Beginning

Eleven Traits of the Best of the Best

1. The Best know what they truly want.
2. The Best want it more.
3. The Best are always striving to get better.
4. The Best do ordinary things better than everyone else.
5. The Best zoom-focus.
6. The Best are mentally stronger.
7. The Best overcome their fear.
8. The Best seize the moment.
9. The Best tap into a greater power than themselves.
10. The Best leave a legacy.
11. The Best make everyone around them better.

Appendixes

Visit www.TrainingCamp11.com to:

- Order *Training Camp* playbooks and coins for you and your organization.

- Print *Training Camp* posters.

- Share the *Training Camp* principles with your organization and team.

- Watch *Training Camp* videos.

- Attend a *Training Camp* event.

Bring Out the Best in Your Team

If you are interested in leadership, sales, and team-building programs based on the *Training Camp* principles, contact the Jon Gordon Companies, Inc., at:

Phone: (904) 285.6842

Email: info@jongordon.com

Online: www.JonGordon.com

Sign up for Jon's free weekly newsletter at www .jongordon.com.

f Facebook.com/JonGordonPage

@JonGordon11

To purchase bulk copies of *Training Camp* for large groups or your organization at a discount, please contact your favorite bookseller or Wiley Special Sales at specialsales@wiley.com or (800) 762-2974.

THE
ENERGY BUS
TRAINING PROGRAM

TRAINING TOOL TO FUEL YOUR LIFE, WORK, AND TEAM WITH POSITIVE ENERGY

The Energy Bus Training Program is an innovative online training platform to help you and your team harness the power of positive energy.

- A 60-minute course featuring an **animated video** retelling of The Energy Bus story, and video commentary by Jon Gordon himself
- Interactive exercises tied to each module
- A customized action plan to help you implement Jon Gordon's 10 Rules and fuel your life, work, and team with positive energy
- Lessons to enhance your positivity and performance
- Management tools to organize and track the progress of your team

Powerful. Scalable. Enjoyable. **The Energy Bus Training Program** is an energizing vehicle for transporting your organization to new heights of accomplishment.

Get on The Bus today!

You and your team will be glad you did.

Learn more at **energybustraining.com**

...y is a registered trademark of John Wiley & Sons, Inc.

WILEY

Other Books by Jon Gordon

The Energy Bus

A man whose life and career are in shambles learns from a unique bus driver and set of passengers how to overcome adversity. Enjoy this enlightening ride of positive energy that is improving the way leaders lead, employees work, and teams function.
www.TheEnergyBus.com

The Energy Bus for Kids

This illustrated children's adaptation of the bestselling book *The Energy Bus* tells the story of George, who, with the help of his school bus driver Joy, learns that if he believes in himself, he'll find the strength to overcome any challenge. His journey teaches kids how to overcome negativity, bullies, and everyday challenges to be their best.
www.EnergyBusKids.com

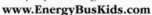

The No Complaining Rule

Follow a VP of human resources who must save herself and her company from ruin, and discover proven principles and an actionable plan to win the battle against individual and organizational negativity.
www.NoComplainingRule.com

The Shark and the Goldfish

Delightfully illustrated, this quick read is packed with tips and strategies for responding to challenges beyond your control in order to thrive during waves of change.
www.SharkandGoldfish.com

Soup

The newly anointed CEO of a popular soup com pany is brought in to reinvigorate the brand and bring success back to a company that has fallen on hard times. Through her journey, discover the key ingredients to unite, engage, and inspire teams and create a culture of greatness.
www.Soup11.com

The Seed

Go on a quest for the meaning and passion behind work with Josh, an up-and-comer at his company who is disenchanted with his job. Through Josh's cross-country journey, you'll find surprising new sources of wisdom and inspiration in your own business and life.

www.Seed11.com

The Positive Dog

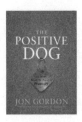

We all have two dogs inside of us. One dog is positive, happy, optimistic, and hopeful. The other dog is negative, mad, pessimistic, and fearful. These two dogs often fight inside us, but guess who wins the fight? The one you feed the most. *The Positive Dog* is an inspiring story that not only reveals the strategies and benefits of being positive but also highlights an essential truth for humans: Being positive doesn't just make you better. It makes everyone around you better.

www.feedthepositivedog.com

One Word That Will Change Your Life

The idea behind *One Word That Will Change Your Life* is a simple concept that delivers a powerful life change! This quick read will inspire you to simplify your life and work by focusing on just one word for this year. *One Word That Will Change Your Life* creates clarity, power, passion, and life change. When you find your word, live it, and share it, your life will become more rewarding and exciting than ever.

getoneword.com